MY
EASY
ISMS

Alex Lienard
Certified ISO 27001 Lead Auditor

ABOUT THE AUTHOR

The author, an expert in information security and risk management, brings a diverse and extensive background in the field. With over twenty years of experience and a passion for information security, the author has worked with organizations of all sizes to implement effective security strategies.

With a deep understanding of the security challenges faced by organizations, the author has made it a priority to make complex information security concepts accessible to all. Through his book, *"My Easy ISMS,"* he offers a practical approach for creating and implementing an Information Security Management System (ISMS) by following clear, guided steps.

With a constant commitment to continuous improvement and the protection of vital information, the author aims to help readers navigate the complex world of information security and establish effective security measures. His expertise and dedication to sharing valuable insights make this book an essential resource for anyone looking to strengthen their information system's security.

CONTENTS

FOREWORD

Originally written in French, this English version was produced by ASPIC PUBLISHING.

1. INTRODUCTION

A. The importance of Information Security

Over time, in our increasingly connected world, information security has become a critical concern for anyone engaged in enterprise, including the public sector. Hardly a week goes by without news reporting a hospital attacked, an emergency service down, or a government office disrupted by hacking. Thus, the private sector, public administrations, NGOs, and non-profit organizations alike all face similar risks as prime targets for cybercriminals.

Gone are the days when one could claim not to be a target or of interest! Today, criticality is no longer the exclusive concern of critical infrastructures (water, energy distribution, telecommunications, etc.). All entities, including individuals, are affected by data theft. Whether it's strategic information or personal data, information security is essential for those who seek to live securely.

Data protection is widely discussed—by large companies, governments, heads of state, and industry leaders—but in practice, few truly invest in it. Yet businesses and organizations store significant amounts of sensitive

1

information, such as banking details, medical records, and trade secrets. What entity doesn't hold this type of data? If this information falls into the wrong hands, the consequences can be disastrous for both the company and those affected. From privacy breaches to identity theft, personal consequences can be severe. Not to mention trade secrets, confidential margins, and other information gems that proliferate across both the mainstream Web and the darknet.

Information system security should play a decisive role in preserving organizational reputation, yet it often does not. Imagine a company experiencing a data breach that becomes publicized. We all remember the hacks at Sony and TV5 Monde. Customer trust is quickly shaken, as is that of business partners. The loss of customers, legal disputes, and negative fallout can significantly impact a company's financial standing.

Information security is also tied to regulatory compliance. Many industries, such as finance, healthcare, and government services, are subject to strict security and privacy regulations. Failure to comply with these regulations can result in fines, legal sanctions, and even business shutdowns.

Information security also supports business continuity. Cyberattacks, system failures, or natural disasters can disrupt operations. By implementing appropriate measures, such as regular backups and disaster recovery plans, organizations can prepare to face such situations and minimize disruptions.

Implementing information security management is therefore essential to protect both sensitive and non-sensitive data, maintain reputation, comply with regulations, and ensure business continuity.

Whether for large enterprises, public administrations, or

SMEs, information security should be a priority to protect systems, prevent financial losses, maintain stakeholder trust, and ensure continuity.

Large enterprises handle massive volumes of information, such as financial data, trade secrets, and development plans. A security breach in a large company can have far-reaching impacts. For example, an e-commerce company suffering a data breach may expose thousands of customers' payment information, resulting in a loss of trust, lawsuits, and a likely significant drop in customer base. Information security is thus essential to protect strategic assets, preserve the company's reputation, and maintain customer confidence.

Public administrations manage vast amounts of sensitive information, including citizens' personal records, tax data, and national security information. Information security is important for ensuring the confidentiality, integrity, and availability of this information. For instance, a security breach in a public administration could lead to the exposure of sensitive citizen data, impacting personal privacy and trust in government. Additionally, attacks on critical infrastructures, such as electoral systems or communication networks, can compromise national security. Information security in public administrations is thus essential to protect citizens' interests and ensure the state's smooth functioning.

Small and medium-sized enterprises (SMEs) often believe they are less likely to be targeted by attacks, but they should not underestimate the importance of information security. Often serving as subcontractors, SMEs also handle sensitive information, such as client data, financial information, and business plans. A security breach can have disastrous financial consequences for an SME. For example, if a professional services firm loses critical data due to a cyberattack, it may experience operational disruptions, contract losses, and a decline in customer trust. SMEs must understand that information security is a important investment to protect their data, maintain customer trust, and ensure long-term viability.

In the urban sector, **connected cities (smart cities)** represent the future, where information and communication technologies are already integrated to improve citizens' quality of life and urban management. However, with this increased connectivity and the rise of the Internet of Things (IoT) across sectors of our economy and private lives, new information security challenges emerge. These challenges are becoming more pressing.

One of the primary concerns is privacy protection. With the mass collection of data from IoT sensors (both public and private), surveillance cameras, social networks, and other sources, it is imperative to ensure that individuals' personal information is handled securely and traceably. New regulations will likely emerge to oversee the collection, use, and storage of such data while respecting citizens' fundamental privacy rights. However, even this may not suffice against the boundless creativity and increasing expertise of cybercriminals.

Cybersecurity is another critical issue in tomorrow's cities, not solely because of the widespread use of IoT. Critical infrastructures in these cities, such as power grids, transport systems, communication networks, and urban management systems, become potential targets for hackers. It is thus essential to establish robust security measures to protect these vital infrastructures from cyber threats. This involves not only technical measures, such as identity and access management, continuous network monitoring, early anomaly detection, and rapid incident response, but also governance solutions tailored to the risks involved.

It is indeed in the technical domain where the difference will be made. Smart cities generate such a vast amount of data from various sources that one can only hope investments will align with the criticality of these issues. It is already essential to implement effective systems and processes to manage, store, analyze, and use this data securely and responsibly. Data must be protected against unauthorized access and misuse while ensuring its integrity and availability for informed decision-making and optimal urban planning.

The widespread arrival of IoT across sectors of our economy and private lives also raises questions about the challenges it creates and modifies. IoT devices, such as security cameras, smart thermostats, voice assistants, and connected health devices, are becoming increasingly present in our daily lives. It is essential to ensure the security of these devices to prevent cyberattacks and privacy violations. Manufacturers and service providers must implement adequate security measures, such as regular software updates, strong passwords, and secure communication protocols.

Simultaneously, the standardization and interoperability of IoT devices with the "old world" is a source of concern and mystery. With the proliferation of devices from different manufacturers, it is essential to establish standards and interoperability protocols now to ensure seamless and secure communication between these devices. Standardization will likely facilitate the implementation of consistent security measures and guarantee a more secure future. This future is already a reality in some mega-cities and capitals.

B. Risks Associated with Cybercrime and Data Breaches

Cybercrime and data breaches increasingly present major risks. The consequences of such incidents can be devastating for individuals, companies, and organizations.

Here are the main risks associated with cybercrime and data breaches:

a) **Theft of Sensitive Information:** Cybercriminals often target sensitive data, such as personal information, banking data, trade secrets, or strategic information. Theft of such information can lead to severe consequences, including privacy violations, identity theft, commercial fraud, and financial losses for both individuals and companies.

b) **Interruption of Business or Industrial Operations:** Cyberattacks, such as ransomware, can paralyze a company's IT systems, resulting in business or production stoppages. This can lead to significant financial losses, productivity drops, and damage to the company's reputation.

c) **Reputation Damage:** Data breaches and cyber incidents can severely harm a company's or organization's reputation. When a company fails to protect its clients' sensitive data, it can result in a loss of trust, withdrawal from clients and business partners, and contribute to negative publicity. Rebuilding a brand's image can be a long and costly process.

d) **Financial Fraud and Theft:** Cybercriminals employ various techniques to steal money, such as hacking bank accounts, phishing, and online scams. These fraudulent activities cause substantial financial losses for both individuals and businesses, and victims may struggle to recover their money.

e) **Disruption of Critical Infrastructure:** Critical infrastructures, such as electrical grids, transportation systems, and water services, are increasingly interconnected with external networks, exposing them to heightened cyberattack risks. A successful attack on these infrastructures can lead to major disruptions, essential service outages, and serious consequences for public safety.

f) **Intellectual Property Theft:** Cybercriminals and state actors may target companies to steal trade secrets or other intellectual property. This can devastate a company's competitiveness and innovation, as well as its market advantage.

g) **Regulatory Non-Compliance:** Data breaches can also lead to regulatory sanctions and heavy fines. Numerous regulations, such as the General Data Protection Regulation (GDPR) in Europe, impose strict obligations for protecting personal data. Non-compliance can result in severe financial and legal consequences.

h) **Physical Risks:** Cyberattacks can sometimes have physical repercussions, especially in the context of connected cities. For example, critical infrastructures, such as power plants or transport systems, may be exposed to targeted cyberattacks aiming to cause malfunctions or outages. This can lead to major disruptions in essential services, endanger public safety, and cause material damage.

i) **Internal Hacking:** Internal hacking risks are a growing concern. Studies indicate that up to 70% of hacking incidents originate internally. Employees with privileged access to company systems and data may misuse their positions to access, disclose, or alter sensitive information. Internal hacking activities can significantly harm a company, compromising data confidentiality and employee trust.

j) **Employee Data Theft:** Employees may also steal sensitive data for personal use, to sell to malicious third parties, or simply out of vengeance. This may include confidential customer information, business strategies, manufacturing secrets, and research and development data. Such data theft can lead to significant financial, legal, and operational impacts for the victimized company or organization.

k) **Digital Social Conflicts:** Digital tools and social media platforms can amplify social conflicts, sometimes even within an organization's information system. Online attacks, harassment, misinformation, and harmful content dissemination can negatively affect individuals, groups, and even society. Companies must take measures to protect employees, maintain a healthy work environment, and manage risks related to digital social conflicts.

l) **Online Harassment:** Digital connectivity also facilitates online harassment, such as cyberbullying, social media harassment, or stalking behaviors. These forms of harassment can inflict significant psychological, emotional, and social harm on targeted individuals, requiring appropriate prevention, education, and protective measures.

Not to be overlooked is a sometimes less-known, even misunderstood category: **industrial espionage.**

Although rarely covered in the media, industrial espionage is a reality and poses a serious threat to companies, particularly in the digital age. Competitors, state actors, and cybercriminal groups may engage in industrial espionage to steal coveted trade secrets, strategic information, and sensitive commercial data. Here are some of the risks associated with industrial espionage:

m) **Loss of Competitive Advantage:** Industrial espionage can result in the loss of valuable competitive advantages. Trade secrets, development plans, marketing strategies, patents, and innovative technologies may be stolen and used by competitors. This can diminish the company's ability to stand out in its markets, impact innovation, or maintain its competitive position.

n) **Reduced Research and Development Effectiveness:** Companies often invest significant resources in research and development to create new products, services, or technologies. Industrial espionage can compromise these efforts by giving third parties access to confidential information on ongoing research projects, leading to significant financial losses and delays in product launches.

o) **Financial and Economic Impact:** Industrial espionage activities can have a considerable financial impact on companies. Costs related to securing and restoring stolen data, securing systems and networks, legal proceedings, and lost revenue can be substantial. Moreover, at a macroeconomic level, industrial espionage can weaken national economies by reducing innovation and competitiveness.

p) **Reputation Damage:** Companies victimized by industrial espionage can suffer significant reputational damage. Public disclosure of data theft or sensitive information can erode trust among clients, business partners, and the public. It can also lead to litigation, contract losses, and difficult public relations challenges.

q) **Threat to National Security:** In some cases, industrial espionage, particularly on a large scale or within the context of asymmetric warfare, can also threaten national security. Stolen information can be used for malicious activities, such as endangering critical infrastructures, disrupting government operations, or compromising national projects. This underscores the importance of collaboration between companies and government agencies to prevent and detect industrial espionage activities.

C. An ISMS, what for?

An Information Security Management System (ISMS) is an integrated management framework designed to protect the availability, confidentiality, and integrity of information within an organization. It provides a structured approach that enables an organization to systematically manage information security risks and implement appropriate controls to mitigate these risks.

An ISMS is based on a set of policies, procedures, practices, and security standards established to ensure the protection of the information system. It enables the identification and assessment of security risks, the definition of security objectives, and the implementation of suitable protective measures.

The main elements of an ISMS include:

a) **Identification of Information System Assets:** It is essential to understand the purpose and nature of the information system, as well as the data and information that are transmitted, created, stored, or managed within it. This also involves identifying assets that make up the information system, such as users, access credentials, computers, mobile phones, copiers, servers, cloud services, industrial computing, etc.

b) **Risk Assessment:** A risk assessment must be conducted to identify threats to the system and vulnerabilities that could compromise information security. This helps in prioritizing security needs and implementing appropriate protection and detection measures.

c) **Definition of Security Policies:** Security policies are established to define the rules and principles that guide the protection of information and systems. This includes policies on information access, password management, data classification, security awareness, and more.

d) **Implementation of Security Controls:** Appropriate security controls are implemented to protect assets. This can include technical measures such as data encryption, firewalls, antivirus solutions, as well as organizational measures such as employee training, access management, and system monitoring.

e) **Incident Management:** An incident management process must be in place to respond effectively to security incidents. This includes detection, analysis, response, and recovery of services after a security incident.

f) **Audit and Evaluation:** Regular audits should be conducted to assess the effectiveness of the information security management system. This allows for identifying gaps, implementing corrective actions, and ensuring the system is constantly evolving positively.

D. Benefits of an ISMS for Risk Mitigation

An ISMS provides numerous benefits for mitigating risks associated with cybercrime, data breaches, and other threats to information security. Some of these benefits include:

a) **Proactive Risk Management:** An ISMS enables a structured and proactive approach to managing information security risks. It offers a methodology for identifying, assessing, and addressing specific risks facing an organization. By identifying vulnerabilities and implementing suitable security measures, an ISMS helps reduce the risk of cyberattacks, data breaches, and other security incidents.

b) **Enhanced Protection of Sensitive Data:** An ISMS

provides a framework for protecting sensitive data, whether internal or related to the organization's stakeholders. Through policies, procedures, and the implementation of adequate controls, an ISMS helps prevent unauthorized access, disclosure, or modification of data, thus significantly reducing exposure to data theft, industrial espionage, and other forms of cybercrime.

c) **Regulatory Compliance:** An ISMS helps organizations meet regulatory requirements for information security. International standards, such as ISO 27001, provide a recognized framework for establishing and maintaining an effective ISMS. By implementing a standards-compliant ISMS, organizations demonstrate their commitment to information security, facilitating compliance with both local and international regulations.

d) **Improved Resilience:** Implementing an ISMS strengthens organizational resilience against security incidents. Through preventive measures, incident response plans, and recovery processes, an ISMS helps minimize operational disruptions in the event of a cyberattack or digital disruption. This enables the organization to react quickly, reduce negative impacts, and resume normal activities sooner.

e) **Strengthening Stakeholder Confidence:** By implementing an ISMS, organizations demonstrate their commitment to protecting information security. This enhances the trust of customers, business partners, and various stakeholders, both external and internal, solidifying relationships.

f) **Security Culture:** Lastly, an ISMS fosters a strong security culture within the organization. By raising employee awareness of the importance of information security and providing them with appropriate training, an ISMS helps reduce risks. By encouraging individual responsibility, it promotes a well-established security culture that forms a solid foundation and unifies users around a common purpose.

In summary, an ISMS offers a proactive and structured approach to mitigating risks associated with cybercrime, data breaches, and other information security threats. It enables the protection of sensitive data, supports regulatory compliance, improves resilience against security incidents, strengthens stakeholder trust, and promotes a security-conscious culture within the organization.

E. Key factors for success

By implementing the following key success factors, you can establish and maintain a robust ISMS (Information Security Management System) that effectively protects your assets and mitigates information security risks.

a) **Management Commitment:** Management's commitment and support are essential for the ISMS's success. Management must recognize the importance of information security, provide the necessary resources, and promote a security-focused culture within the organization. This commitment helps create positive momentum and ensures buy-in at all levels of the company.

b) **Risk Assessment:** Thorough risk assessment is the cornerstone of an ISMS. Identifying critical information assets, vulnerabilities, threats, and their potential impacts is essential. This risk assessment guides decisions on implementing appropriate security measures and helps prioritize actions to be undertaken.

c) **Clear Policies and Procedures:** Establishing clear security policies and procedures is fundamental to operating an effective ISMS. Detailed security policies outlining the goals and principles to follow should be developed, communicated, and implemented organization-wide, aligned with the project's defined scope. Operational procedures (working instructions) should be created to guide employees in applying security policies in practice.

d) **Employee Participation and Awareness:** Active employee participation and awareness of information security are necessary. Providing adequate training on security policies and procedures, promoting a security-focused culture, and encouraging employees to report security incidents are important. Ongoing awareness efforts help establish a security-oriented culture and reduce human-related security risks.

e) **Supplier Management:** Information security extends beyond the organization's boundaries. It is essential to establish supplier management processes to ensure third parties working with the organization also adhere to normative requirements and security best practices. This includes supplier assessments, incorporating security clauses in contracts, and continuously monitoring suppliers' security performance, especially if they interact with the organization's information system.

f) **Monitoring and Evaluation:** An effective ISMS requires regular monitoring and evaluation. Security measures should be assessed and adjusted in response to evolving threats and vulnerabilities. Internal and external audits, penetration testing, and compliance reviews are necessary to ensure the ISMS operates optimally.

g) **Continuous Improvement:** Continuous improvement is a core principle of an ISMS. Establishing a formal process to identify gaps, improvement opportunities, and implement corrective actions is essential. Regularly reviewing policies, procedures, and security controls ensures ongoing, adaptive information security protection.

F. Utility

Large Enterprises

Due to their scale, complexity, and the value of the information they handle, large enterprises face considerable information security risks. An ISMS (Information Security Management System) is invaluable in this context. By providing a structured and methodical framework, an ISMS enables large enterprises to protect their information assets and effectively manage associated risks.

One of the primary uses of an ISMS for large enterprises is in safeguarding sensitive assets. With vast amounts of customer data, trade secrets, financial information, and third-party connections, implementing adequate security measures to protect these assets is essential. The ISMS identifies critical assets, assesses associated risks, and establishes appropriate controls and procedures to ensure their security.

Moreover, an ISMS allows large enterprises to proactively manage information security risks. Through regular assessments of vulnerabilities, threats, and the potential impact of security incidents, these sometimes-sprawling organizations can take preventive measures to mitigate these risks, thus avoiding the financial and operational repercussions of security breaches.

An additional benefit of an ISMS is ensuring regulatory compliance, especially for large multinational organizations exposed to diverse global regulations on data protection, privacy, and security. The ISMS aids large enterprises in adhering to these regulations by implementing policies, procedures, and controls that align with legal requirements, thereby reducing exposure to legal risks, fines, and penalties associated with non-compliance.

Large enterprises also work with a vast network of suppliers and business partners. An ISMS facilitates third-party security management by establishing security criteria for supplier selection, evaluation, and monitoring, ensuring that business partners meet expected security standards while reducing risks associated with information exchanges with potentially unreliable third parties.

Another ISMS advantage for large enterprises is in fostering stakeholder communication and trust. Clients, business partners, shareholders, and the public highly value information security. By implementing a compliant ISMS, large enterprises demonstrate their commitment to information protection and offer transparency regarding the measures in place. This strengthens stakeholder trust and reinforces the company's reputation.

Finally, an ISMS enables large enterprises to manage security incidents effectively. Despite preventive measures, security incidents may still occur. The ISMS establishes clear procedures for detecting, managing, and responding to security incidents, minimizing downtime, operational disruptions, and negative impacts on the business.

Public Sector

The public sector plays a vital role in providing services to citizens and managing sensitive information. Implementing an ISMS offers several benefits for the public sector.

Firstly, an ISMS protects the sensitive and critical information held by public entities. Government agencies manage personal data, medical records, tax and legal information, and numerous other confidential details. By implementing appropriate security controls, such as data encryption, strong authentication, and access management, the ISMS reduces the risks of data breaches and unauthorized disclosures.

An ISMS also provides a proactive approach to managing information security risks. Through regular risk assessments, public entities can identify vulnerabilities and threats to their information activities. By implementing appropriate security measures, they can mitigate these risks and prevent costly security incidents, data losses, and attacks.

Regulatory compliance is another advantage of an ISMS for the public sector. Government agencies are subject to strict regulations on data protection and privacy, such as the General Data Protection Regulation (GDPR) in Europe. An ISMS simplifies compliance by requiring the establishment of policies, security procedures, and controls that meet legal standards and requirements, reducing legal risks and fines associated with non-compliance.

An ISMS also enhances citizen trust in the public sector. By implementing contextually adapted, robust security measures, government entities demonstrate their commitment to protecting citizen data. This strengthens citizens' trust in the management of their personal information, thereby reinforcing the relationship between the public sector and citizens.

Crisis and incident management is another critical function of an ISMS for the public sector. Government agencies may face major crises and incidents that require efficient information security management. An ISMS provides clear procedures for incident management, stakeholder communication, and disaster recovery, enabling a rapid, coordinated response in the event of an incident, thereby reducing negative impacts and service interruptions.

Finally, an ISMS facilitates secure collaboration. The

public sector often engages in partnerships and collaborations with other public entities, international organizations, and private partners. The ISMS establishes security criteria for information exchanges, ensuring that partners adhere to expected security standards, fostering more effective and secure collaboration and strengthening relationships among partners.

Non-Governmental Organizations (NGOs)

NGOs play an important role in promoting human rights, humanitarian aid, environmental protection, and other essential causes. Implementing an ISMS offers several benefits for NGOs, their beneficiaries, and their funders.

Firstly, an ISMS protects NGOs' informational assets. These organizations often handle personal data, confidential information on beneficiaries and projects, as well as strategic and political information. By implementing appropriate security measures, such as access control, data encryption, and employee awareness, the ISMS helps reduce the risk of data breaches and unauthorized disclosures.

Additionally, an ISMS provides a proactive approach to managing information security risks faced by NGOs. Through regular risk assessments, NGOs can identify potential vulnerabilities and threats. By implementing appropriate security controls and measures, they reduce risks and prevent security incidents that could compromise their operations (abroad) and their ability to provide the aid they pledge.

An ISMS also facilitates compliance with international data protection and privacy regulations. NGOs often must adhere to strict confidentiality and data protection standards, especially when handling sensitive personal information. An ISMS helps to establish policies, procedures, and controls that comply with regulatory requirements, reducing legal risks and penalties associated with non-compliance.

Another benefit of an ISMS for NGOs is strengthening stakeholder trust. Donors, beneficiaries, and partners expect NGOs to protect their information and meet prevailing information security standards in their operating environments. By implementing an ISMS, NGOs affirm their commitment to security and information confidentiality, reinforcing trust and credibility among stakeholders.

Crisis and incident management is also a vital function of an ISMS for NGOs, allowing them to address emergencies, natural disasters, or unstable political situations. An ISMS provides clear procedures for managing security incidents, coordinating responses, ensuring continuity, and protecting critical assets during crises.

Small and Medium-sized Enterprises (SMEs)

SMEs often face constraints in resources, budgets, and expertise, making information security management particularly challenging. However, implementing an ISMS offers several advantages for SMEs willing to take the leap.

Firstly, an ISMS helps protect SMEs' assets and ensures business continuity. Even small businesses manage customer data, financial information, or other confidential and sensitive data. By implementing appropriate security measures, such as access management, data backups, and employee awareness, an ISMS reduces the risks of data breaches, information theft, and financial losses.

An ISMS also offers a structured approach to managing information security risks faced by SMEs. By assessing potential vulnerabilities, threats, and impacts, SMEs can identify the areas where they are most exposed and then implement appropriate security measures. This allows them to reduce risks and prevent security incidents that could harm their reputation and business continuity.

An ISMS also facilitates compliance with information management regulations and legal requirements. SMEs must comply with laws and regulations like the General Data Protection Regulation (GDPR) in Europe. An ISMS provides the ideal framework for establishing policies, procedures, and controls in accordance with regulatory requirements, reducing legal risks and fines associated with non-compliance.

Another advantage of an ISMS for SMEs is enhancing customer and business partner trust. By implementing an ISMS, SMEs demonstrate their commitment to protecting sensitive information and business continuity, which reinforces customer and partner trust, potentially strengthening business relationships.

Incident management is also essential for SMEs. Despite security measures, incidents like cyberattacks or data theft can still occur. An ISMS provides clear procedures for incident management, incident response, and disaster recovery, allowing SMEs to react quickly, minimize impacts, and limit activity interruptions.

When SMEs work as subcontractors for larger organizations, they may be required to meet stringent security standards set by the client. This may include protecting confidential information, managing access and rights, and implementing technical and organizational security measures. Without a well-structured ISMS, an SME may struggle to meet these requirements and risk losing business opportunities.

Security Certification as a Growing Requirement for Business Partners and Suppliers

In an increasingly digital and interconnected business landscape, information security has become a primary concern for companies. To protect sensitive data and reduce security risks, more companies now require their partners and suppliers to hold a security certification. This trend underscores the need to strengthen the supply chain and ensure compliance with security standards and regulations.

Large companies increasingly recognize the importance of securing their information systems and the data they handle, including client information, trade secrets, and financial data. However, internal security measures alone are often insufficient to guarantee complete protection. This is why companies increasingly require that their partners and suppliers also uphold high-security standards. A security certification verifies that third parties handle data securely and apply adequate protection measures.

The primary benefit of security certification for partners and suppliers is reducing security risks. By imposing specific standards and controls, organizations requiring certification can ensure their partners adhere to strong security practices, reducing the risk of data breaches, information leaks, or potential attacks. By strengthening the entire chain, they aim to mitigate risks and protect their informational assets in a more controlled environment.

Organizations often operate in complex regulatory environments with stringent laws on confidentiality, data protection, and information security. Security certification enables partners and suppliers to demonstrate compliance with these standards and regulations, facilitating mutual trust and ensuring that information assets are managed responsibly and in line with legal requirements.

When a company requires a security certification from its

partners and suppliers, it sends a clear message: information security is our priority. This requirement demonstrates the company's commitment to data protection and strengthens the trust of clients, investors, and other stakeholders. By working with certified partners, the organization can enhance its reputation as a responsible and reliable actor in information security.

The requirement for security certification can also significantly impact business relationships. Some partners or suppliers may be unwilling or unable to meet certification requirements, leading to more selective partner choices and possibly replacing those that do not meet required security standards. However, this requirement can also foster strong partnerships based on proven mutual trust and a shared understanding of security issues.

2. UNDERSTANDING ISMS FUNDAMENTAL

A. Definition and Objectives of an ISMS

An Information Security Management System (ISMS) is an organized, structured framework that enables organizations to effectively manage the security of their sensitive information. It comprises policies, procedures, practices, and security measures to ensure confidentiality, integrity, and availability of information. The primary objective of an ISMS is to protect sensitive information against internal and external threats, minimize security risks, and preserve business continuity

ISMS Objectives:

a) **Protect Sensitive Information:** One of the primary objectives of an ISMS is to protect sensitive information held by an organization, including customer data, financial information, trade secrets, and any other information considered critical to the company. For example, a bank will implement an ISMS to protect its clients' financial information from cyberattacks and fraud.

b) **Manage Information Security Risks:** The ISMS aims to identify, evaluate, and manage information security risks, allowing an organization to understand threats, vulnerabilities, and the impact of security incidents. For example, a manufacturing company may identify the risk of competitors stealing its product designs and implement security controls such as restricting access to sensitive information and monitoring data flows.

c) **Ensure Regulatory Compliance:** The ISMS helps organizations comply with information security regulations and standards, including specific regulations such as the General Data Protection Regulation (GDPR) in Europe or standards like HIPAA in the healthcare industry. For example, a healthcare company must comply with HIPAA regulations to ensure the confidentiality of patient medical records and will implement an ISMS to meet these requirements.

d) **Strengthen Stakeholder Trust:** By implementing an ISMS, an organization demonstrates its commitment to information security, thereby strengthening trust among its stakeholders, including customers, business partners, investors, and employees. For example, a cloud computing company may obtain ISO 27001 certification to reassure its clients that their data will be protected according to international information security standards.

e) **Effectively Manage Security Incidents:** Another key objective of an ISMS is to enable an organization to manage security incidents in a structured, rapid, and efficient manner. This includes early detection, analysis, response, and recovery after an incident. For example, an e-commerce company may have an incident response plan to handle hacking attempts and minimize service disruptions.

f) **Promote a Security Culture:** The ISMS also aims to promote a culture of security within the organization. This includes raising employee awareness about information security, training on best security practices, and encouraging accountability for protecting information. For example, a company may implement regular training sessions to educate employees on phishing threats and teach them how to identify suspicious emails.

B. Overview of Commonly Used Standards and Frameworks (ISO 27001, NIST, etc.)

In the field of information security, several internationally recognized standards and frameworks provide detailed guidance on implementing an Information Security Management System. These standards and frameworks offer organizations a solid foundation for developing policies, procedures, and implementing security controls tailored to their specific needs. Among the widely used standards and frameworks, ISO 27001 and NIST (National Institute of Standards and Technology) are widely adopted by organizations around the world.

- **ISO 27001:** Published by the International Organization for Standardization (ISO), ISO 27001 is an international standard for information security. It provides a framework for managing information security risks and specifies the requirements for establishing, implementing, operating, monitoring, reviewing, maintaining, and continuously improving an ISMS. ISO 27001 is based on a risk management approach, encouraging organizations to identify risks, evaluate them, and implement appropriate security controls. It also provides guidelines for auditing and certifying compliance with the standard.

- **NIST SP 800-53:** The NIST Special Publication (SP) 800-53 is a security control framework developed by the U.S. National Institute of Standards and Technology (NIST). It provides detailed guidelines for selecting and implementing IT security controls within information systems. NIST SP 800-53 covers a wide range of security areas, such as access management, communication security, configuration management, incident management, and business continuity. It is used by many government agencies and private organizations as a reference for ensuring information security.

In the vast landscape of information security standards and frameworks, it is important to note that there are many options. However, in this book, we will primarily focus on ISO 27001 due to its widespread adoption and comprehensive approach to information security management.

This book focuses on the core principles of the ISMS to facilitate understanding and application of information security concepts. We understand that each organization is unique and may have specific needs and constraints. Therefore, rather than adhering to a single standard or framework, we aim to provide practical advice and general guidelines that can be applied, regardless of the standard chosen by the reader.

The core principles of an ISMS remain largely consistent across different standards, with minor variations in specific details and requirements. Based on these principles, organizations can design and implement their own ISMS tailored to their needs and constraints.

In this book, we will address topics such as risk identification and assessment, implementation of appropriate security controls, incident management, employee awareness, regulatory compliance, and other essential aspects of an ISMS. These principles apply regardless of the chosen standard, as they represent a solid foundation for ensuring information security within an organization.

By providing concrete examples, case studies, and practical advice, our goal is to guide readers in setting up their ISMS, based on core principles and best practices in information security. This will enable readers to understand fundamental concepts and adapt these principles to their own organizational environment, considering the specific standards and requirements applicable to them.

Regardless of the standard chosen by the reader, whether ISO 27001, NIST, or another framework, the core ISMS principles remain relevant and applicable. By following the advice and recommendations presented in this book, readers can develop a strong ISMS tailored to their organization, based on fundamental information security principles.

C. Explanation of Key ISMS Principles

The ISMS is based on three fundamental principles of information security: confidentiality, integrity, and availability (sometimes expanded to include traceability and non-repudiation). These principles form the basis of effective information security management within an organization and are essential for ensuring the protection and proper management of sensitive information.

- **Confidentiality:** Confidentiality is about protecting assets and information from unauthorized access. It ensures that only authorized individuals can access information and that it is not disclosed to unauthorized parties. Confidentiality aims to prevent information leaks, data theft, and privacy breaches. For example, in a financial services company, confidentiality would be essential for protecting clients' financial information from unauthorized access.

To ensure confidentiality within an information system, certain security controls must be implemented, such as access management, data encryption, firewalls, and confidentiality policies. Security awareness and training measures are also required to inform employees about best practices for protecting confidential information.

- **Integrity:** Integrity refers to the accuracy, precision, and completeness of information. It ensures that information is not modified, altered, or destroyed without authorization or accidentally. Integrity is essential for preserving the validity and reliability of information, as well as for preventing malicious alterations that could compromise trust in data. For example, in the healthcare sector, it is essential to maintain the integrity of patient medical records to ensure safe and quality care.

To ensure integrity, the organization implements controls such as change management, data verification, digital signatures, and regular backups. Change management policies and procedures are established to ensure that information remains accurate and unaltered over time.

- **Availability:** Availability refers to ensuring that information and services are accessible and usable when needed. It ensures that IT systems, networks, and services are operational and accessible to authorized users. Availability is essential for maintaining business continuity, avoiding costly interruptions, and providing services reliably. For example, in the e-commerce sector, availability is fundamental to ensure the website and order management tools are accessible.

To ensure availability, the organization implements controls such as business continuity planning, system redundancy, regular backups, and incident management. Disaster recovery tests are conducted to ensure that systems and data can be quickly restored in case of an incident.

The key principles of an ISMS — confidentiality, integrity, and availability — form the foundation for ensuring the desired level of information security. The organization implements controls and measures to ensure the confidentiality of sensitive information, maintain data integrity, and guarantee the availability of systems and services. By understanding and applying these principles, organizations can effectively manage information security risks and maintain a secure and reliable environment.

D. In the Real Life

Examples of Loss of Confidentiality:

- **Data Theft:** A hacker manages to break into a company's computer system and steals sensitive information, such as customer data, financial information, or trade secrets.
- **Accidental Disclosure:** An employee mistakenly sends an email containing confidential information to the wrong person or leaves a sensitive document on a desk accessible to everyone.
- **Data Leak by a Third Party:** A supplier or business partner with access to sensitive information deliberately or accidentally discloses it to third parties, thus compromising confidentiality.
- **Phishing:** Cybercriminals send fraudulent emails with the intent to obtain confidential information, such as login credentials or banking information, by impersonating a legitimate entity.
- **Theft or Loss of Devices:** An employee loses a laptop, USB drive, or smartphone containing classified information, exposing this data to unauthorized access.
- **Brute Force Attacks:** Attackers use automated tools to try different password combinations to guess them and access protected accounts.
- **Unauthorized Access to Shared Files:** An employee accesses shared files or information not intended for them, thus compromising the confidentiality of the affected data.
- **Internal Data Leaks:** A malicious employee copies or transmits confidential information to third parties without authorization, either for financial gain or revenge.
- **Industrial Espionage:** A competing company or

external actor engages in espionage activities (not limited to digital means) to obtain confidential information on an organization's products, business strategies, or manufacturing secrets.

- **Unauthorized Media Disclosure:** Confidential information about a company is disclosed through the media, for example, when a journalist obtains internal documents and publishes them without prior authorization.

Examples of Proposed ISMS Measures for Confidentiality:

The following examples represent some of the commonly used measures to ensure information confidentiality. The implementation of these measures may vary based on each organization's needs and specificities.

- **Access Management:** Implementing controls to limit access to information only to authorized and relevant individuals. This may include the use of strong passwords, multi-factor authentication, and physical access controls.
- **Data Encryption:** Utilizing encryption techniques to protect information during storage and transmission, rendering data unreadable to any unauthorized person attempting to access it.
- **Confidentiality Policies and Procedures:** Developing clear policies and procedures to inform employees of confidentiality obligations and appropriate practices for protecting information.
- **Information Classification:** Classifying information based on its sensitivity and confidentiality level, allowing for the definition of appropriate security measures according to each piece of information's classification level.
- **Employee Training and Awareness:** Regularly training employees on best practices for confidentiality, threats,

and protection measures, contributing to a security culture and fostering employee accountability.

- **Information Sharing Controls:** Implementing strict controls over information and data sharing, whether internally within the organization or with external partners. This may include confidentiality agreements, secure transfer protocols, and mechanisms for tracking access and usage.
- **Physical Security:** Securing physical premises where sensitive information is stored by using strong locks, alarm systems, surveillance cameras, and other physical security measures to prevent unauthorized access.
- **Vendor Management:** Evaluating the security of suppliers and partners with whom the organization shares information. This may include controls to ensure that vendors adhere to the same information security standards.
- **Data Anonymization:** Utilizing anonymization techniques to remove or mask personally identifiable information from data sets, thereby protecting individuals' privacy.
- **Audit and Monitoring:** Conducting regular internal and external audits to assess the effectiveness of information security measures and detect any potential confidentiality breaches. Continuous monitoring enables a rapid response in the event of an incident.

Examples of Loss of Integrity:

The following examples highlight various situations where data integrity can be compromised, whether due to malicious attacks, human errors, or technical failures. It is necessary for organizations to implement appropriate security measures to prevent these integrity losses and ensure data reliability.

- **Unauthorized Data Modification:** An attacker intentionally modifies data stored in a database or information system, altering its integrity. This may

31

include changing financial amounts, customer contact details, or test results.

- **Data Corruption:** Storage errors, hardware failures, or malicious attacks can lead to data corruption, rendering it unusable or affecting its accuracy.
- **Unauthorized Data Insertion:** An attacker inserts unwanted or malicious data (virus) into a system or database, compromising the integrity of existing data. For example, inserting false information into an inventory management system could cause tracking and management issues.
- **Distributed Denial of Service (DDoS) Attacks:** Attackers flood a system or network with illegitimate traffic, potentially causing outages or slowdowns that affect data integrity and service availability.
- **System File Alteration:** Malicious software modifies essential system files on a computer, potentially leading to malfunctions, errors, or data loss.
- **Communication Manipulation:** Attackers intercept and modify communications between parties, which may result in altered messages, content changes, or transaction manipulations.
- **Malicious Code Injection:** Attackers exploit application vulnerabilities to inject malicious code, which can alter data, corrupt systems, or compromise overall security.
- **Physical Document Alteration:** Important paper documents may be altered, forged, or modified, compromising the integrity of the information they contain, including contracts, financial reports, or legal documents.
- **Data Alteration During Transmission:** Data may be altered or modified during transmission over unsecured networks, especially if encryption measures are not in place.
- **Human Errors:** Human errors, such as incorrect

data entry or accidental manipulations, can also lead to data integrity losses.

Examples of Proposed ISMS Measures for Integrity:

The following examples represent some of the recommended measures for ensuring data integrity within an ISMS. It is essential to select appropriate measures according to each organization's needs and specifics.

- **Access and Authentication Controls:** Implementing robust authentication mechanisms such as strong and complex passwords, multi-factor authentication, and role-based access controls to ensure that only authorized individuals' access and modify data.
- **Cryptography:** Using encryption techniques to protect data integrity during storage and transmission, enabling verification of data authenticity and detection of any unintended alteration.
- **Change and Version Control:** Establishing change management processes to ensure that modifications made to systems and data are controlled, documented, and approved, preventing unauthorized or undocumented changes that could compromise data integrity.
- **Input Validation Controls:** Implementing validation controls to verify the reliability and validity of incoming data, helping prevent entry errors and malicious data injection attempts.
- **Logging and Monitoring:** Setting up logging and monitoring mechanisms to track system activities and detect any suspicious or unauthorized data modifications, allowing for quick detection of alteration attempts and identification of those responsible.
- **Configuration Management:** Adopting configuration management practices to ensure that systems and applications are correctly configured and that changes are made in a controlled manner, helping prevent

incorrect configurations that could compromise data integrity.

- **Regular Backups:** Performing regular data backups to prevent data loss in the event of an incident and to restore data in case of corruption or alteration.
- **Penetration Testing:** Regularly conducting penetration tests to assess the resilience of systems and applications against attacks targeting data alteration, allowing for the identification of vulnerabilities and implementation of appropriate corrective measures.
- **Separation of Functions:** Implementing mechanisms to separate functions and responsibilities related to data management and modification to avoid conflicts of interest and reduce the risk of unauthorized changes.
- **Employee Training and Awareness:** Regularly educating employees on best practices for information security, particularly regarding data handling and modification, contributing to promoting a security culture and strengthening vigilance among all.

Examples of Loss of Availability:

The following examples highlight various situations where the availability of data and services may be compromised. It is essential for organizations to implement preventive and mitigation measures to minimize availability risks and maintain business continuity.

- **Distributed Denial of Service (DDoS) Attacks:** An attacker targets an organization's IT systems by overwhelming them with illegitimate traffic, overloading resources, and rendering services unavailable to legitimate users.
- **Hardware or Software Failures:** Technical failures, such as server crashes, configuration errors, or software bugs, can result in service interruptions and data unavailability.
- **Human Error:** Human errors, such as accidental data

deletion, system handling mistakes, or configuration errors, can lead to data or service unavailability.

- **Natural Disasters:** Events such as fires, floods, storms, or earthquakes can damage IT infrastructure and cause service interruptions.
- **Ransomware Attacks:** Attackers use malicious software to encrypt an organization's data and demand a ransom for decryption. This can lead to data unavailability until the ransom is paid or data is restored from backups.
- **Service Provider Outage:** If an organization relies on services hosted by an external provider, an outage at that provider may lead to service unavailability for the organization.
- **Backup and Restoration Errors:** If backup and data restoration procedures are not properly implemented, errors may occur, leading to data unavailability in the event of failure or corruption.
- **Unauthorized System Access:** If unauthorized individuals manage to access an organization's systems or accounts, they may disrupt services, modify configurations, or delete data, resulting in service unavailability.
- **Network Connectivity Issues:** Network issues, such as equipment failures, configuration errors, or connectivity problems, can make services inaccessible to users.
- **Planned Maintenance:** Scheduled maintenance periods, when improperly managed or communicated, may result in service unavailability for users.

Examples of Proposed ISMS Measures for Availability:

These examples illustrate some of the recommended measures for ensuring data and service availability within an ISMS. It is important to tailor these measures according to each organization's needs and constraints, ensuring they meet availability and business continuity requirements.

- **Business Continuity Planning:** Developing a business continuity plan that identifies critical processes, defines backup and disaster recovery measures, and establishes procedures to minimize interruptions and maintain service availability.
- **System Redundancy:** Implementing redundant systems and automatic failover mechanisms to ensure continuous service availability in the event of hardware or software failures.
- **Regular Backups:** Performing regular data backups to prevent data loss in the event of an incident and facilitate restoration to quickly restore data availability.
- **Patch and Update Management:** Establishing a process for managing updates and patches to ensure continuous system availability by applying security patches and keeping software up to date.
- **Incident Monitoring and Management:** Setting up proactive monitoring of systems and networks to quickly detect incidents and outages and implementing effective incident management to minimize downtime and restore service availability.
- **Capacity Planning:** Evaluating and planning IT infrastructure capacity to ensure it can handle the expected workload and maintain optimal performance without compromising service availability.
- **Physical Security Controls:** Implementing physical security measures, such as surveillance systems, access controls, and fire protection systems, to protect hardware infrastructure and minimize availability loss risks due to physical incidents.
- **Change Management:** Applying change management processes to ensure that modifications made to systems, networks, and applications are well planned, tested, and documented to reduce the risk of incidents and availability disruption.
- **Disaster Recovery Testing:** Regularly conducting disaster recovery tests to evaluate the effectiveness of backup and recovery plans, identify necessary

improvements, and ensure rapid service availability after an incident.

- **Service Level Agreements (SLAs):** Establishing contractual agreements with external service providers to define expected availability levels and ensure reliable service delivery according to agreed requirements.

3. STEP 1: ESTABLISHING THE CONTEXT

A. Identification of Stakeholders and Their Expectations

When implementing an Information Security Management System (ISMS), it is strongly recommended to identify stakeholders and understand their expectations regarding information security. For ISO 27001 certification, this is even a mandatory requirement. Stakeholders are individuals or groups who have a direct or indirect interest in the information security of an organization. This may include employees, customers, suppliers, business partners, regulatory authorities, and even society.

a) **Identification of Stakeholders:** The first step is to identify the relevant stakeholders for the organization. This can be achieved through a careful inventory of stakeholders, identifying people or groups directly or indirectly affected by the organization's activities or who are connected to the organization's information system. It is important to consider all actors, both internal and external, who impact the organization's information security.

- **Employees:** Employees are one of the key stakeholders,

as they are directly involved in the day-to-day management of information security and are often the primary actors responsible for data protection.

- **Customers:** Customers are also important stakeholders, as they expect their personal or confidential information to be handled carefully and protected from unauthorized access or leaks.
- **Suppliers and Partners:** Suppliers and business partners are often involved in processing and storing information. Ensuring they adhere to information security standards, objectives, principles, and measures is essential to reduce risks related to the supply chain.
- **Regulatory Authorities:** Regulatory bodies may have specific expectations regarding information security, particularly in highly regulated sectors such as healthcare, finance, or telecommunications. This is also true for organizations and companies working directly or indirectly in sectors deemed critical by governments.

b) **Understanding Stakeholder Expectations:** Once stakeholders are identified, it is necessary to understand their expectations regarding information security. This can be achieved through interviews, surveys, or regular exchanges with the relevant stakeholders.

- **Confidentiality:** Stakeholders often expect their personal or sensitive information to be handled confidentially and not disclosed to unauthorized third parties.
- **Integrity:** Stakeholders expect data to be accurate, complete, unaltered, and protected from unauthorized or unexpected manipulation.
- **Availability:** Stakeholders expect services and information to be available when needed, without extended interruptions or downtimes.
- **Regulatory Compliance:** Stakeholders may have specific expectations concerning compliance with applicable information security laws, regulations, or

standards.

- **Trust and Reputation:** Stakeholders attach great importance to trust and reputation. They expect the organization to take appropriate measures to prevent security incidents and protect their data.

By understanding stakeholder expectations, the organization can establish information security objectives that meet these expectations and implement appropriate measures to satisfy these requirements. This approach helps build trust, reduce risks, and establish strong relationships with stakeholders involved in information security. Third-party security and the protection of their informational assets may form an inherent security objective within the established relationship.

Examples of Stakeholder Identification and Their Expectations

These examples illustrate the diversity of stakeholders and their expectations regarding information security. It is essential to consider these expectations when designing and implementing an ISMS to meet the needs of all stakeholders and enhance the organization's trust and reputation.

- **Employees:** Employees expect their personal information to be protected, their access to systems to be secure, and to receive training on best practices in information security.
- **Customers:** Customers expect their personal and financial data to be handled confidentially, protected against unauthorized access and leaks, and to trust the security of the organization's services and products.
- **Suppliers and Partners:** Suppliers and partners expect the organization to protect the sensitive information they share, maintain the confidentiality of their commercial data, and adopt information security practices that comply with standards and regulations.

- **Regulatory Authorities:** Regulatory authorities expect the organization to comply with applicable laws and regulations regarding information security, particularly in terms of personal data protection, financial information confidentiality, and security risk management.
- **Shareholders and Investors:** Shareholders and investors expect the organization to implement strong information security measures to protect assets and sensitive information, reduce security-related risks, and maintain stakeholder confidence.
- **Standards and Certification Bodies:** Standards and certification bodies expect the organization to comply with recognized information security standards and frameworks, such as ISO 27001, and to implement appropriate security practices to obtain certification or accreditation.
- **Public Opinion and Society:** Society and public opinion expect the organization to protect personal and sensitive information, be transparent about its information security practices, and respond appropriately in the event of a security incident to maintain public trust.

Depending on the chosen standard, methods and requirements may vary. Below is an example of how the NIST and ISO suggest addressing this specific issue.

The **National Institute of Standards and Technology (NIST)** is a U.S. agency responsible for developing and promoting standards and guidelines in information systems. Although NIST does not provide a specific definition of stakeholders in its publications, it acknowledges the importance of stakeholders in the context of information security management.

In documents such as NIST SP 800-53 (Security and Privacy Controls for Federal Information Systems and Organizations) and the **NIST Cybersecurity Framework**, stakeholders are implicitly addressed. These documents emphasize the importance of identifying stakeholders, their interests, and their information security requirements.

NIST encourages organizations to consider internal and external stakeholders during the planning, implementation, and management of information security programs. This includes identifying key stakeholders such as users, managers, IT teams, regulators, customers, suppliers, etc. The needs and expectations of these stakeholders must be considered to ensure effective risk management and adequate information protection.

While NIST does not have a publication specifically focused solely on stakeholders, it encourages organizations to adopt a holistic approach to information security by actively involving stakeholders in the security planning and implementation process.

It is important to note that NIST provides general recommendations and guidelines. Organizations must tailor these recommendations based on their specific needs and the regulations applicable to their sector.

ISO/IEC 27001:2022 is the most widely recognized international standard for information security management. It provides a framework for establishing, implementing, maintaining, and improving an Information Security Management System (ISMS) within an organization.

ISO 27001 recognizes the importance of stakeholders in information security management. It encourages organizations to identify and consider both internal and external stakeholders, as well as their expectations and requirements.

According to ISO 27001, stakeholders may include customers, employees, business partners, suppliers, regulatory authorities, standards organizations, shareholders and investors, and society at large. The standard emphasizes understanding these stakeholders' needs and expectations to ensure information security measures are appropriate and meet their expectations.

ISO 27001 requires (for certification purposes) organizations to conduct a stakeholder analysis to identify key stakeholders, understand their information security expectations, and determine how their needs can be met. This analysis provides a better understanding of information security issues and enables informed decisions regarding appropriate security measures.

ISO 27001 provides a general framework for information security management, allowing organizations to customize and adapt security measures based on their specific needs and environment. Consequently, each organization can define its own stakeholders and take their specific expectations into account when designing and implementing its ISMS, in line with ISO 27001 principles and requirements.

B. Internal and External Environment Analysis

Analyzing the internal and external environment is a key step in implementing an Information Security Management System (ISMS). This analysis allows for an understanding of the strengths, weaknesses, opportunities, and threats related to information security within the organization. A comprehensive analysis helps identify the internal and external factors that may impact the level of information security, enabling well-informed decisions to protect the organization's information assets.

a) Internal Environment Analysis:

- **Human Resources**: Assessing employees' skills, knowledge, and awareness of information security, including identifying roles, training, and the security culture within the organization.

- **Technological Infrastructure**: Evaluating systems, networks, equipment, and software used to process, store, and transmit sensitive information, including identifying vulnerabilities, weaknesses, and the need for upgrades or enhanced security.
- **Policies and Procedures**: Reviewing existing security policies, procedures, and practices to evaluate their adequacy, compliance with information security standards, and effectiveness in protecting information assets.
- **Incident Management**: Assessing mechanisms for detecting, responding to, and recovering from information security incidents, including identifying reporting processes, tracking, and continuous improvement.
- **Technologies Used in the Information System**: Analyzing the systems, platforms, and technological services in use, which includes assessing vulnerabilities, security practices, and the risks associated with using these technologies.

b) External Environment Analysis:

- **Regulatory Framework**: Evaluating laws, regulations, and information security standards applicable to the organization and its operational scope, including identifying legal and regulatory requirements and compliance obligations.
- **External Threats and Risks**: Analyzing external threats, such as cybercrime, hacking, industrial espionage, and the evolving techniques and trends in information security, to understand the risks the organization faces.
- **Partners and Suppliers**: Evaluating relationships with business partners, suppliers, and service providers, including identifying supply chain risks and implementing appropriate security controls.
- **Competitive Environment**: Analyzing competitors' information security practices and their potential impact

on the organization to understand industry standards and identify best practices to adopt.

- **Technologies Used by External Stakeholders**: Analyzing the systems, platforms, and technological services used by external stakeholders, including assessing vulnerabilities, security practices, and the risks associated with using these technologies.

The internal and external environment analysis provides an overall view of the current state of information security and factors that may influence its effectiveness. This in-depth understanding allows for informed decision-making and prioritization when implementing appropriate security measures within the ISMS framework.

Tools and Techniques for Analyzing the Internal and External Environment

Analyzing the internal and external environment when implementing an Information Security Management System (ISMS) can be conducted using various tools and techniques. Here are some commonly used tools for this analysis:

- **SWOT Analysis (Strengths, Weaknesses, Opportunities, Threats)**: The SWOT model is an analysis tool used to identify the strengths, weaknesses, opportunities, and threats related to information security within the organization. It helps evaluate internal resources, capabilities, gaps, and external factors that may influence information security.
- **Risk Analysis**: Risk analysis is a structured method for identifying, evaluating, and prioritizing risks associated with information security. It involves identifying information assets, assessing threats and vulnerabilities, and estimating the potential impact of security incidents. Techniques such as quantitative risk analysis, qualitative risk analysis, and risk assessment matrices may be used for this analysis.

- **Process Analysis**: Process analysis aims to understand the activities and information flows within the organization, identifying vulnerability points, dependencies between processes, and existing security measures. Techniques such as process flow diagrams, process mapping, and value chain analysis can be used in this analysis.
- **Policy and Procedure Review**: Reviewing existing policies and procedures related to information security is essential to assess their adequacy, compliance with standards and regulations, and effectiveness in protecting information assets. Document reviews and benchmarking against best practices can be used for this review.
- **Regulatory Compliance Study**: Studying legal and regulatory requirements applicable to the organization is essential to assess compliance in information security. This may include identifying laws, industry regulations, and security standards, and evaluating the adequacy of existing information security practices in relation to these requirements.
- **Past Incident Review**: Reviewing past security incidents can provide valuable insights into potential gaps and issues related to information security. It helps identify recurring vulnerabilities, process errors, human errors, and previous corrective measures, aiding in avoiding similar incidents and strengthening information security.

These tools and techniques can be used complementarily to obtain a comprehensive picture of the organization's internal and external environment. The analysis should be conducted regularly and iteratively to adapt to internal and external changes that may impact information security.

Data Collection in External Relations

Data collection in the context of external relations can

quickly become a seemingly insurmountable challenge, but several approaches and methods can help overcome these obstacles effectively. Here are some strategies that can be used to collect data from external stakeholders:

- **Questionnaires and Surveys**: Questionnaires and surveys are commonly used tools to collect data from external stakeholders. They can be sent by email, postal mail, or even administered online (be mindful of confidentiality aspects). Design clear, concise, and relevant questionnaires to gather specific information on the expectations, needs, and perceptions of external stakeholders regarding information security.
- **Interviews**: Face-to-face or telephone interviews with external stakeholders are an effective method for gathering detailed information. These can be structured or semi-structured, allowing for specific questions and in-depth responses. Interviews can be conducted with customers, suppliers, business partners, or other key external stakeholders.
- **Contract and Agreement Reviews**: Reviewing contracts, agreements, and existing security policies with external stakeholders can provide valuable information about their expectations and requirements for information security. These documents may reveal security clauses, regulatory compliance requirements, confidentiality commitments, etc.
- **Consultations and Meetings**: Organize consultations or meetings with representatives of external stakeholders to discuss their expectations and concerns about information security. This may include regular meetings with key clients, discussions with suppliers during contract establishment, and meetings with regulatory bodies.
- **Market Studies and External Research**: Market studies and external data research can provide insights into best practices, industry trends, customer expectations, and applicable regulations. Consult reliable

sources, such as analyst reports, industry publications, and case studies, to obtain relevant data.

- **Collaborations and Working Groups**: Engage in collaborations with other organizations in the same sector or specialized working groups to share information on common information security challenges. This can facilitate the exchange of best practices, experiences, and knowledge among external stakeholders.

It is essential to take a proactive and transparent approach when collecting data from external stakeholders. Ensure compliance with confidentiality and data protection requirements during data collection and processing.

Addressing Confidentiality Concerns in Data Collection

When internal or external relationships invoke confidentiality to withhold information during data collection, it is important to take certain steps to address this situation:

- **Raising Awareness on the Importance of Information Security**: Clearly and persuasively explain the importance of information security and why you wish to collect data. Highlight the benefits for the organization and stakeholders involved. Show how a better understanding of risks and expectations in information security can strengthen trust, prevent security incidents, and improve operational processes.
- **Confidentiality of Collected Data**: It is critical to reassure stakeholders regarding the confidentiality and protection of the collected data. Demonstrate transparently, with supporting evidence, how information will be processed, stored, and protected in accordance with applicable regulations. Implement appropriate security measures to ensure data confidentiality and comply with the organization's

privacy policies.

- **Offering Alternatives**: If a stakeholder refuses to provide certain information for confidentiality reasons, suggest alternatives that may address their concerns while still allowing you to gather useful data. This may include using aggregated or anonymized information, excluding sensitive data, or using data from third-party sources or external references.

- **Confidentiality Agreements**: If necessary, establish ad hoc confidentiality agreements with the stakeholders concerned to protect the exchanged confidential information. These agreements can define each party's rights and obligations regarding confidentiality and data protection, allowing for information exchange in full confidence.

- **Independent Experts**: In some cases, it may be helpful to enlist independent experts or external consultants to conduct information security assessments or collect sensitive data impartially and confidentially. These experts can provide additional expertise and help establish a climate of trust with stakeholders.

- **Compliance with Regulations and Standards**: Ensure compliance with applicable regulations and standards regarding confidentiality and data protection. Make sure that your data collection practices conform to the legal and regulatory requirements, which can help build stakeholder trust.

In all situations, maintain open and transparent communication with stakeholders and respect their concerns regarding confidentiality and other security-related aspects. By adopting this respectful and balanced approach, it is possible to gather relevant information while maintaining mutual trust and respect.

C. Defining the ISMS Scope

Defining the ISMS (Information Security Management

System) scope allows for setting boundaries and measuring the extent of the ISMS. This ensures that resources and efforts are focused on relevant areas, facilitating effective risk management and the protection of the organization's information assets.

The qualification of the ISMS scope is a key step in implementing an Information Security Management System. It involves clearly defining the boundaries and size of the ISMS, covering the activities, processes, services, systems, and information included in the ISMS scope. The following steps are recommended:

a) Identify Linked Assets Included in the Information System

The first step is to identify the organization's information assets, encompassing all assets of value to the organization, whether physical or digital, structured or unstructured. This includes:

- **Data**: such as customer data, financial data, trade secrets, strategic plans, intellectual property, etc.
- **Systems**: including servers, software, databases, mobile devices, network equipment, etc.
- **Organizational**: such as user accounts, organizational charts, procedures, and intangible assets.

b) Define Activities and Processes

Define the organization's activities and processes included in the ISMS scope, such as business operations, provided services, production processes, human resources management processes, etc. This step helps to better understand information flows, vulnerability points, and risks associated with each activity.

c) Identify Relevant Stakeholders

Identify internal and external stakeholders directly involved in the activities included in the ISMS scope. This may include employees, customers, suppliers, business partners, regulators, etc. Involving all relevant stakeholders is essential to ensure effective information security management.

d) Establish Physical and Logical Boundaries

Define the physical and logical boundaries of the ISMS:

- **Physical Boundaries**: specify geographic locations, sites, physical facilities where activities take place, and systems are hosted.
- **Logical Boundaries**: specify digital limits such as networks, IT systems, applications, databases, etc.

e) Consider External Stakeholders

It is also important to consider interactions with external stakeholders impacting the organization's information security. This includes exchanges with suppliers, subcontractors, business partners, clients, cloud service providers, etc. Establishing appropriate agreements and controls is essential to ensure that information security is considered in relationships with these external stakeholders.

f) Document the ISMS Scope

Once the ISMS scope is determined, it is essential to document it clearly and precisely. This can be done by developing an information security policy that specifies the ISMS scope, identifying the included information assets, covered activities, and relevant stakeholders.

By following these guidelines, you can appropriately determine the ISMS scope while considering internal and external factors affecting information security. This helps focus efforts on critical areas and establishes a strong foundation for your Information Security Management System.

- **Involve Stakeholders**: Ensure the involvement of all relevant stakeholders in defining the scope, including representatives from various departments, IT teams, regulatory compliance, as well as key suppliers and partners. Their perspectives and insights contribute to a better understanding of activities and risks related to information security.
- **Analyze Information Flows**: Conduct an in-depth analysis of information flows within the organization, identifying key processes and activities involving the collection, processing, storage, and transmission of sensitive information. This will help identify critical areas where information security needs strengthening.
- **Evaluate Information and Their Flows**: Exhaustively identify information essential to the organization's operation, including customer data, financial data, trade secrets, strategic information, intellectual property, flows, transfer areas, etc. Assess the importance and sensitivity of each type of information to determine its appropriate inclusion in the ISMS scope.
- **Consider Regulations and Standards**: Consider applicable regulations and standards relevant to your organization. Ensure you understand information security requirements, particularly concerning personal data protection, financial confidentiality, industry compliance, etc., and include these areas within the ISMS scope.
- **Account for Sites and Systems**: Identify physical sites, network infrastructures, IT systems, applications, and databases used in the organization's activities. Establish physical and logical boundaries to delineate systems and networks included in the ISMS scope.
- **Assess External Stakeholders**: Consider suppliers, subcontractors, business partners, and external service

providers with access to the organization's sensitive information. Ensure appropriate controls and agreements are in place to manage information security risks in these relationships.

Examples of Determining the ISMS Scope

The following examples illustrate how different organizations might define the scope of their ISMS based on their activities, information assets, and involved stakeholders. Customizing the scope is essential to meet the specific needs of each organization while considering regulations, standards, and industry-specific requirements.

- **An Online Retail Business**: An online retail business needs to define its ISMS scope by considering key information flows. This may include customer data collection activities, order processing, online payment systems, customer databases, web applications, etc. Important information assets might include customer personal data, payment information, and order details. Relevant stakeholders may include customers, employees, payment service providers, logistics partners, etc.
- **A Healthcare Company**: A healthcare company should define its ISMS scope by considering sector-specific regulations. This may include activities related to the collection, storage, and transmission of medical information, electronic health record management systems, access management processes, etc. Important information assets might include patient medical records, personal health information, and medical test results. Relevant stakeholders may include patients, healthcare professionals, regulatory bodies, insurers, etc.
- **A Financial Institution**: A financial institution needs to define its ISMS scope by considering key activities related to financial information security. This may include online banking operations, transaction

processing, account management systems, customer databases, etc. Important information assets might include account information, customer financial data, and credit card information. Relevant stakeholders may include customers, employees, financial regulators, payment service providers, etc.

4. STEP 2: RISK EVALUATION

A. Risk Theory

Introduction

In our increasingly connected and technology-driven world, information security has become a critical concern for organizations of all sizes and industries. Information security risks are pervasive and can have devastating consequences for organizations, from the loss of confidential data to breaches of individuals' privacy, damage to corporate reputations, and disruptions in business or industrial operations.

Information security encompasses the protection of information assets, specifically data, whether stored electronically or in physical form. The nature of this information makes it an attractive target for cybercriminals, hackers, industrial spies, rogue states, and even certain malicious employees.

Information security risks are varied and constantly evolving alongside technological advancements. Cybercrime is one of the most concerning threats of our time, with its array of sophisticated attacks aimed at stealing information, blocking systems, or causing significant financial damage, if not resorting to financial blackmail. Data breaches, where confidential information is compromised, are also a major concern for organizations as they can lead to financial loss, lawsuits, and erosion of trust among partners.

With the advent of smart cities and the expansion of the Internet of Things (IoT) across all sectors of our economy and private lives, new risks emerge, often inadequately accounted for. Connected systems and devices offer new opportunities for health and convenience but are also vulnerable to attacks, endangering the confidentiality, integrity, and availability of information and services we rely on.

Faced with these challenges, organizations must take proactive measures to mitigate information security risks. This is where the implementation of an Information Security Management System (ISMS) comes in. And without risk management, there can be no ISMS.

In this more theoretical section on information security, we will explore the various risks that organizations face, the potential consequences of these risks, and best practices for mitigating them. We will also delve into conducting risk analysis and its key factors.

By developing a thorough understanding of information security risks and taking a proactive approach to managing them, organizations can strengthen their resilience, protect their information assets, and build the trust necessary to thrive in an ever-evolving digital world.

What is a Risk?

In information systems security, a risk is defined as the possibility of an undesirable event occurring that will likely result in negative consequences. It is the uncertainty around the occurrence of an event that could cause damage, loss, or unwanted impacts. In this specific context, a risk is related to the possibility of harm or incidents that could compromise the confidentiality, integrity, or availability of the information system, in part or in full.

Typically, a risk is characterized by the combination of two key elements: the probability of the undesirable event occurring and the potential impact associated with this event. Probability represents the likelihood of the event happening, while impact represents the severity of the consequences should the event occur.

It's worth noting that not all risks are negative. Some risks also present opportunities and advantages. In the context of information security, it is essential to consider both negative and positive risks. For instance, implementing new technologies may introduce security risks but also improve operational efficiency and present new business opportunities.

Risk management involves proactively identifying, assessing, and addressing risks. This includes taking steps to reduce the probability of undesirable events, minimize potential impact, or avoid them altogether. Organizations implement risk management strategies to identify risks, assess their significance, make informed decisions on control measures, and continually monitor risks to ensure they are effectively managed.

Risk management in information security is a continuous, iterative process. Organizations must regularly evaluate risks, mitigate them with appropriate measures, and periodically reassess the effectiveness of these measures. This helps maintain an adequate level of security and ensure the protection of information against potential threats and incidents.

When it comes to addressing risks, there are different

strategies available, depending on the nature of the risk, its potential impact, and the organization's risk appetite. Here are some commonly used approaches:

- **Reduce**: This strategy aims to reduce the probability or impact of identified risks. It involves implementing security controls, policies, and procedures, as well as adopting good risk management practices. For example, deploying firewalls to reduce the risk of cyber-attacks or training employees to reduce human error or phishing exposure.
- **Transfer**: This strategy involves transferring part or all the risk to a third party, such as an insurance company or external provider. This can be done through contracts, insurance policies, or business partnerships. For example, an organization may transfer the risk of data loss to a data backup and recovery company.
- **Avoid**: This strategy entails completely avoiding the risk by abstaining from certain activities, removing processes, or abandoning high-risk projects. This may be used when risks are deemed unacceptable or when the costs associated with managing them are disproportionate to the expected benefits, financial or otherwise.
- **Accept**: This strategy involves accepting the risk without taking specific measures to address it. This may be used when the cost of reducing or transferring the risk is prohibitive or when the risk is considered acceptable given potential benefits or its low probability of occurrence.

These strategies are not mutually exclusive and may be combined depending on the circumstances and the organization's objectives. Risk management is a continuous process that requires regular risk evaluation, informed decision-making, and adaptation to organizational and environmental changes, especially within an ISMS.

Identifying and implementing appropriate risk treatment

strategies is essential to protecting the organization's assets, ensuring business continuity, and achieving the established goals. Each decision must be made with consideration of costs, benefits, legal and regulatory obligations, as well as the organization's values and risk tolerance.

There are also many myths surrounding risk management, particularly concerning the role of the CISO (Chief Information Security Officer). Their role is not limited to making unilateral decisions on managing information security risks. The CISO acts as an expert advisor responsible for providing recommendations and technical solutions to mitigate risks and enhance information security within the organization.

The CISO works closely with top management, to whom they typically report, as well as with executive leadership and organizational stakeholders to assess risks, develop security policies, and propose appropriate protective measures. However, it is ultimately top management's responsibility to make the final decisions regarding risk management, whether related to information security or other areas such as business, financial, legal, or operational risks.

The CISO plays a key role in raising awareness of information security issues and establishing security practices and standards within the organization. They are responsible for providing accurate risk information, assessing potential consequences, and recommending adequate security measures. However, the final decision on how to handle risks and the organization's priorities lies with top management, which must evaluate information security concerns considering business, financial, operational, and strategic factors.

This approach ensures that decisions related to information security are made in a balanced manner aligned with the organization's overall goals and interests. It involves close collaboration among stakeholders and informed decision-making based on a comprehensive understanding of risks, costs, benefits, and organizational constraints.

Managing information security risks requires close collaboration between the CISO and the organization's top management. This collaboration enables the sharing of relevant information, recommendations, and responsibilities, allowing informed decisions that protect the organization's overall interests.

The CISO, as an information security expert, brings technical expertise and an in-depth understanding of risks to assess vulnerabilities, identify threats, and propose appropriate protective measures. They play a key role in raising security awareness and developing risk management policies and procedures.

Top management, as the strategic decision-maker, ultimately holds the responsibility of making informed decisions on risk management. They must evaluate risks considering the organization's strategic objectives, budget constraints, and operational concerns.

The collaboration between the CISO and top management ensures that information security objectives are aligned with the organization's overall goals. It fosters a shared understanding of risks and potential impacts, supports informed decision-making based on best practices, and ensures appropriate resource allocation for effectively managing risks.

Working together, the CISO and top management can develop a coherent, integrated approach to risk management, ensuring that security measures align with organizational priorities. They can also promote a risk management culture in which all members of the organization understand their role and responsibility in protecting information. For effective collaboration, continuous and transparent engagement is essential.

Sometimes you may hear about risk acceptance criteria and accepted risks, meaning that the organization has established predefined thresholds or limits to determine which risks are acceptable and which need mitigation or avoidance.

Risk acceptance criteria are generally based on a prior, thorough assessment of potential impacts, occurrence probabilities, and consequences associated with risks. They may vary from organization to organization based on risk tolerance, strategic objectives, and specific considerations related to the company's environment and industry.

When a risk is deemed acceptable, it means the organization has chosen to tolerate it rather than take measures to reduce or eliminate it. It will not be fully transferred, either. This may be due to various factors, such as high mitigation costs, limited impact on activities, or the possibility of transferring the risk in full to a third party.

Accepting a risk does not mean it is ignored or neglected—quite the opposite. Accepted risks must be regularly monitored to ensure they remain within tolerance levels and periodically reassessed.

Risk acceptance criteria and accepted risks should be clearly defined and documented to guide risk management decisions and provide a solid foundation for the organization's future activities.

The Value of a Combined Approach

Success in analyzing information security risks often lies in the mixed use of several complementary methods. Each method offers a different perspective and helps cover a wide range of risks. By using a combination of these methods, organizations can achieve a deeper, more realistic understanding of risks, enabling them to make the most informed and suitable decisions. Here are some examples of mixed use of risk analysis methods:

- **Quantitative and Qualitative Risk Analysis**: Combining these two approaches allows organizations to assess risks more precisely and with nuance. Quantitative analysis provides numerical data and measurements, while qualitative analysis enables a more subjective assessment and classification of risks based on severity and probability. By using both methods, organizations gain a comprehensive view of risks. This dual perspective helps them make sound decisions based on both quantitative data and qualitative judgments.
- **Attack Scenario Method and Vulnerability Assessment**: Attack scenarios simulate realistic situations to better understand the potential consequences of attacks, while vulnerability assessment identifies weaknesses and potential exploit points in the information system. By combining these two methods, organizations can pinpoint the most critical and likely scenarios based on existing vulnerabilities. The measures and controls implemented are then highly contextualized.
- **Defense-in-Depth Risk Analysis and Best Practices Study**: Defense-in-depth analysis helps understand the protective layers established within the organization. Additionally, studying best practices allows for identifying effective security measures used by similar organizations. By combining these two approaches, organizations can evaluate their existing controls against industry best practices and identify improvement areas to strengthen their security posture.
- **Industry-Specific Methods and Regulation-Based Analysis**: In some cases, organizations may use methods specific to their industry or based on the regulations to which they are subject. For instance, in the healthcare sector, using risk analysis methods compliant with HIPAA standards can be essential. By combining these sector-specific methods with broader approaches,

organizations can address sector-specific risks while maintaining a holistic view of information security.

Using a mixed approach and combining risk analysis methods allows organizations to achieve more comprehensive, precise, and tailored results. This enables them to make informed decisions to mitigate information security risks effectively and proactively.

Determining Occurrence

Assessing the likelihood, or probability, of a risk event is a complex process that depends on the specific context of the organization and the risks being considered. Here are several approaches and methods to evaluate the probability of a risk occurring:

- **Historical Data Analysis**: Analyzing historical data on past incidents can provide insight into the frequency and probability of risks occurring. By examining past incidents, trends, and patterns, it is possible to estimate the likelihood of future occurrences. However, it's worth noting that this method relies on the assumption that past conditions are like the present context.
- **Experience and Expertise of Professionals**: Information security professionals with in-depth knowledge of the organization, its processes, and its environment can offer their expertise to assess the likelihood of risks occurring. They draw on their experience, understanding of current and emerging threats, and knowledge of existing vulnerabilities and controls in place.
- **Benchmark Studies and External Sources**: Benchmark studies, industry reports, or reliable external sources can provide insights into the probability of very specific risks. These sources often include reports from standards organizations, market studies, government agencies, or academic research. These external data

sources can support and supplement internal assessment. Used alone, however, such studies rarely provide a comprehensive view and seldom reflect an organization's internal and external context.

- **Expert Group Evaluation**: The organization can bring together a group of internal or external experts to collectively assess the likelihood of risks occurring. Experts can share their perspectives and estimates based on their specific experience and expertise. This approach can yield more comprehensive assessments and consider diverse viewpoints.

- **Scoring and Ranking Methods**: Scoring and ranking methods can be used to assign numerical values or scores to the probability of risks occurring. This may involve using scales, matrices, or specific rating models. Scoring criteria can be defined based on the organization's specific characteristics and the risks being considered.

It is essential to note that assessing the probability of risks typically involves estimates and judgments and may therefore contain an element of subjectivity. It is recommended to document the methods used, sources of information, and assumptions considered to ensure transparency and reproducibility of evaluations. Probability assessments should also be regularly reviewed to account for changes in the environment and new information.

Determining Impact

Determining the impact of a risk is a critical step in risk analysis. Impact represents the potential consequences of an undesirable event on the organization. Here are some factors to consider when determining risk impact:

- **Assessing Direct Consequences**: Identify the direct consequences of an undesirable event on various aspects of the organization, such as confidentiality, integrity, availability of information, reputation, business operations, regulatory compliance, finances, etc. Evaluate consequences in terms of financial losses, downtime, loss of productivity, customer loss, loss of trust, regulatory penalties, etc.

- **Assessing Indirect Consequences**: Consider indirect consequences that could arise from the initial impact. For example, a security incident leading to customer data loss may have immediate financial consequences, but also damage the organization's long-term reputation, resulting in loss of customers and new business opportunities.

- **Severity Assessment**: Assess the severity of consequences based on their potential impact on the organization. This may include qualitative assessments, such as low, moderate, high, or critical impact, or quantitative assessments, such as estimated financial losses, expected downtime, number of affected customers, etc.

- **Duration of Impact Assessment**: Consider the potential duration of the impact on the organization. Some risks may have short-term consequences, while others may have longer-term effects. For instance, a ransomware attack blocking data access may result in immediate downtime, but residual effects like customer trust loss may persist longer.

- **Scope Assessment**: Assess the scope of impact regarding the area or parts of the organization that could be affected. This could range from limited disruption to a specific department to a broader impact affecting the entire organization.

Evaluating the impact of a risk can be subjective and will depend on the organization's specific context. It is essential to involve key stakeholders and use factual data where possible to support the assessment. Clear documentation of evaluation criteria and assumptions is also important to ensure consistency and transparency in the evaluation.

How to Define a Risk Scale?

A risk scale is a tool used to assess and rank risks according to their severity. It provides a standardized method for quantifying and comparing different risk levels that an organization faces. A risk scale assigns a numerical value or category to each risk, facilitating understanding and communication of associated risk levels.

A risk scale is generally based on predefined criteria, such as the probability of an undesirable event and its potential impact on the organization. These criteria can vary depending on each organization's specific needs and preferences.

The main purpose of a risk scale is to enable a systematic risk assessment to better prioritize management and control measures. By assigning a value or category to each risk, decision-makers can identify the most critical risks and allocate the necessary resources to manage them appropriately qualified and quantified.

Implementing a risk scale also aids decision-making by providing clear benchmarks for evaluating the acceptability of the associated risks. Additionally, it quickly determines if a given risk should be accepted, mitigated, or avoided based on its severity level. This helps guide risk management efforts by focusing on the most significant risks, ensuring efficient allocation of resources.

Lastly, using a risk scale offers benefits in terms of communication and information sharing. A common scale enables various stakeholders within the organization to easily understand the relative severity of identified risks and the measures planned to address them. Harmonized scales also allow for integrating information security risk management into other organizational risk categories.

It's worth noting that the risk scale should be tailored to each organization's specific needs. Probability, impact, and classification criteria vary significantly depending on activities, operational context, and organizational requirements.

When using a risk scale, a common question is whether it's preferable to use even-numbered (e.g., a 1 to 4 scale) or odd-numbered measures (e.g., a 1 to 5 scale). While there's no definitive answer, there are a few considerations to keep in mind.

One of the main advantages of using even-numbered measures is the potential for a more decisive evaluation. With an even-numbered scale, you have sharper evaluation degrees, leading to a less median evaluation. The error vectors are then called pessimism or optimism.

On the other hand, odd-numbered measures can facilitate decision-making and avoid indecision or ambiguity during risk assessment. With an odd-numbered scale, there's often a temptation to aim for the midpoint (3 on a 1 to 5 scale), which can discourage evaluators from taking a clear stance.

Ultimately, the choice between even- or odd-numbered measures depends on each organization's specific needs and the context of the risk assessment. Some prefer a more detailed, granular approach, while others prioritize simplicity and decisiveness.

Whichever approach is chosen, it is essential to ensure that risk scales are consistent, understood, and used uniformly throughout the organization. This ensures coherent risk assessment and facilitates comparison and aggregation of results.

Setting up a Risk Scale and Management Approval

Establishing a risk scale and securing management's

approval are two essential steps to ensure effective risk management within an organization. Here are some phases to follow for setting up a risk scale and obtaining management's approval:

a) **Establish Measurement Criteria**: Define the specific criteria on which the risk scale will be based. These criteria may include factors such as the probability of an undesirable event, potential impact on the organization, and other relevant factors. Ensuring that criteria align with the organization's goals and needs is essential.

b) **Develop the Risk Scale**: Create a graduated scale to quantify risk levels. You can use a numerical scale (e.g., 1 to 10) or a category-based scale (e.g., low, medium, high). Ensure that the scale is detailed enough to reflect the various nuances of risks the organization faces.

c) **Evaluate Existing Risks**: Use the risk scale to assess existing risks within the organization. Apply the defined criteria to each identified risk to rank them on the scale, providing an initial assessment of risk levels.

d) **Review and Adjust the Scale**: Based on the results of the risk assessment, review and adjust the risk scale as necessary. Ensure that it aligns with identified risk levels and allows for accurate and relevant assessment.

e) **Present the Risk Scale to Management**: Prepare a presentation of the risk scale, highlighting the criteria used, corresponding risk levels, and the scale's importance in the organization's risk management. Provide a detailed explanation of the methodology used and the benefits of using this scale.

f) **Obtain Management Approval**: Arrange a meeting with management to present the risk scale and obtain their approval. Explain the importance of the scale in making informed decisions and in managing risks consistently and systematically. Address any questions or concerns they may have.

g) **Integrate the Risk Scale into Processes**: Once the risk scale is approved by management, ensure it is integrated into the organization's risk management processes. Use the scale systematically to assess risks, make decisions, prioritize mitigation actions, and communicate effectively about risk levels.

Note: Establishing a risk scale and securing management's approval are iterative processes. The scale may need adjustments and improvements over time to meet the organization's evolving needs and accurately reflect risk levels.

The Difference between "Risk Assessment" and "Risk Analysis"

Risk assessment and *risk analysis* are two distinct yet closely related terms within the risk management process.

- **Risk Assessment**: Risk assessment is the process of identifying, analyzing, and evaluating risks for the organization. It involves identifying risks, evaluating their probability of occurrence and potential impact, and then ranking them by severity. The goal of risk assessment is to provide a comprehensive understanding of the risks the organization faces, enabling informed decisions on risk management. Typically, risk assessment involves the following steps:
  - o **Risk Elements Identification**: This entails identifying potential threats, vulnerabilities, and weak points within the organization's systems, processes, and activities.
  - o **Risk Scenario Determination**: This involves establishing risk scenarios by asking questions like who, what, how, why, and when?
  - o **Risk Analysis**: Once risk scenarios are

identified, they are analyzed by evaluating their probability and potential impact, which can be done qualitatively or quantitatively using methods such as qualitative or quantitative risk analysis (see above).

- o **Risk Evaluation**: Risks are then evaluated by ranking them according to severity, probability, and impact. This prioritizes risks and allows focus on the most critical ones or those that require immediate attention.

- **Risk Analysis**: Risk analysis focuses on the detailed examination and assessment of the risks identified during the risk assessment. It involves an in-depth analysis of the causes and potential consequences of risks to understand their impact on the organization better. Risk analysis aims to provide detailed information to make informed decisions on control measures and risk management strategies. Risk analysis can include the following elements:

  - o **Cause Analysis**: This step involves identifying factors and events contributing to the occurrence of risks. For example, in the case of a cyberattack, causes may include system vulnerabilities, human errors, security flaws, or external attacks.

  - o **Consequence Analysis**: This involves evaluating the potential impacts of risks on the organization. Consequences may be financial, operational, regulatory, reputational, etc.

  - o **Control Measure Analysis**: This step involves assessing the effectiveness of existing or proposed control measures to mitigate risks. It helps determine whether control measures are adequate or if improvements are necessary.

Though *risk assessment* is the overall process of identifying and evaluating risks, while *risk analysis* is a more detailed step that focuses on the in-depth analysis of identified risks. Risk analysis provides key information for making informed decisions on control measures and strategies to implement.

B. Risk Assessment Methodologies (Analysis of Vulnerabilities, Threats, Impact)

Risk assessment methodologies are essential in information security management as they help identify, analyze, and evaluate risks that an organization may face. Here are some of the most used methodologies:

- **Vulnerability Analysis**: This approach focuses on identifying weaknesses, security flaws, and potential exploitation points in systems, networks, infrastructure, or even in the organization's processes. It can be performed using techniques such as penetration testing, vulnerability scanning, code reviews, or security audits. The goal is to understand specific vulnerabilities that could be exploited by threats.
- **Threat Analysis**: Threat analysis aims to identify and assess the various threats that could affect an information system. These threats may include cyberattacks, human errors, natural disasters, acts of sabotage, etc. Threat analysis helps understand potential attack or incident scenarios and determine their likelihood.
- **Impact Analysis**: Impact analysis evaluates the potential consequences of risks on the organization. This could include financial losses, operational disruptions, reputational damage, confidentiality breaches, or compliance issues. Impact analysis quantifies the consequences and helps prioritize risks based on their severity.
- **Qualitative Assessment Methods**: These methods use rating scales, risk matrices, or rankings to evaluate risks based on predefined criteria. For instance, a rating scale might assess a risk's probability and impact, assigning an overall score to determine risk criticality.
- **Quantitative Assessment Methods**: Quantitative

methods rely on available numerical data and models relevant to the issue at hand. This may involve probability calculations based on statistics, cost-benefit analyses, Monte Carlo simulations, or other quantitative techniques. These methods provide more precise risk estimates, but they generally require reliable data and additional resources.

Note: Organizations may choose different methodologies depending on their needs, the complexity of their information systems, the scope of the ISMS, available resources, and specific regulatory requirements. A mixed approach combining several methodologies often produces more comprehensive and precise results in risk assessment. Regardless of the chosen methodology, it is important to document the results and rationales to ensure transparency and reproducibility in the risk assessment process.

Choosing the Right Method

Selecting the appropriate risk analysis method depends on several factors, including the nature of the risks, available resources, the organization's context, and regulatory requirements. Here are some key elements to consider when choosing a risk analysis method:

- **Nature of Risks**: Understand the nature of the risks your organization faces. Some risks may be more technical and specific to IT security, while others may be more related to regulatory compliance, information system governance, business continuity, or other organizational aspects. Identify key areas where risks are located and look for methods best suited to these areas.
- **Complexity Level**: Consider the complexity of the risks and the organization. Some risk analysis methods may be simpler and faster to implement, while others may be more complex and resource intensive. Assess your internal capabilities, risk management expertise, and available resources to determine if a simpler or more in-

depth method is appropriate.

- **Available Resources**: Evaluate available resources, particularly in terms of time, skills, and budget. Some risk analysis methods require specific expertise, dedicated software, or specialized tools, while others can be performed with internal resources and simpler tools. Choose a method that is realistic given the resources at hand.

- **Regulatory Requirements**: Review regulatory and standard requirements applicable to your organization. Some industries or jurisdictions may mandate specific risk analysis methods or require adherence to mandatory frameworks. Ensure you choose a method that complies with these requirements and meets the expectations of regulatory authorities.

- **Organizational Preferences**: Consider your organization's specific preferences and needs. Some methods may be better suited to your organizational culture, management style, or strategic goals. Consider internal stakeholder opinions and preferences to select a method aligned with your organization's values and priorities.

Note: You may combine different risk analysis methods for a more comprehensive and thorough understanding. Some organizations use a hybrid approach, adapting methods to meet their specific needs. It is advisable to become familiar with the various risk analysis methods, consult experts in the field, and leverage industry best practices to help choose the right method.

Examples of Methods

There are numerous methods and tools available for identifying, evaluating, and even managing risks. These approaches offer structured frameworks that help organizations understand and manage the risks they face effectively. Let's briefly explore this range of methods and tools.

One of the most widely used methods is risk analysis, which involves identifying and evaluating risks considering threats, vulnerabilities, and consequences. Risk analysis methods vary from qualitative approaches, using rating scales and risk matrices, to quantitative approaches, using numerical data and mathematical models to assess probabilities and impacts.

Popular methods include **ISO 27005, OCTAVE, MEHARI, NIST SP 800-30**, and **FMEA**. Each of these methods offers a specific approach for identifying, evaluating, and prioritizing risks, focusing on different aspects such as primary assets, supporting assets, threats, vulnerabilities, and impacts.

Beyond these specific methods, there are also risk management tools that facilitate the process of identifying and evaluating risks. These tools often provide features such as data collection, risk analysis, result visualization, and report generation. Some tools are designed specifically for fields, such as industrial IT, cloud environments, regulatory compliance, or business continuity management.

It is essential to note that each method and tool has its own advantages and disadvantages. Choosing the right method or tool will depend on the organization's specific needs, risk complexity, available resources, and regulatory requirements. Combining several methods or tailoring approaches to an organization's specific needs can also be beneficial.

Regardless of the chosen method or tool, it is important to understand that risk identification and assessment are iterative and evolving processes. They should be regularly reviewed and updated to consider new risks, organizational environment changes, and newly acquired knowledge and skills. Clear communication and smooth collaboration between stakeholders are also decisive to ensure the effectiveness of these methods and tools.

The variety of methods and tools available for identifying and evaluating risks provides flexibility for organizations to choose the approach that best suits their needs. Selecting methods and tools should be based on risk characteristics, available resources, and specific organizational requirements.

- **ISO 27005 Risk Analysis**: Based on the ISO/IEC 27005 standard, this method follows a structured approach to risk assessment. It involves identifying assets, threats, vulnerabilities, and potential impacts, as well as estimating the probability of risks occurring. This method uses risk matrices to prioritize risks and recommend appropriate treatment measures. Its appendix provides an example that many companies use.
- **OCTAVE Method**: Developed by the CERT Coordination Center at Carnegie Mellon University, OCTAVE (Operationally Critical Threat, Asset, and Vulnerability Evaluation) focuses on identifying critical assets, specific threats, and vulnerabilities within the organization. OCTAVE uses group workshops to encourage collaboration among stakeholders and generate recommendations for improving security measures. It provides a highly contextualized theoretical approach.
- **MEHARI Method**: Developed by the French information security club CLUSIF, MEHARI (*Méthode harmonisée d'analyse de risques*) focuses on identifying assets, threats, and vulnerabilities, as well as estimating the impact and probability of risks. MEHARI uses a scenario-based approach to assess consequences and prioritize risks.
- **NIST SP 800-30 Risk Analysis**: Proposed by the National Institute of Standards and Technology (NIST) in its Special Publication 800-30, this method follows an approach based on identifying assets, threats,

vulnerabilities, impacts, and probabilities. NIST SP 800-30 risk analysis uses risk matrices to assess risk levels and identify appropriate treatment measures.

- **FMEA (Failure Mode and Effects Analysis) Method**: Primarily used in engineering and manufacturing, FMEA can also be applied to information security risk analysis. It involves identifying potential failure modes, assessing their severity, likelihood, and detectability to prioritize risks and establish preventive measures.

These examples represent a selection of the most used methods. It is important to note that many other methods and approaches are available, such as scenario analysis, the Delphi method, fault tree analysis (FTA), and more. The choice of method will depend on the specific needs of your organization and available resources.

Example Using the EBIOS Risk Management Methodology

EBIOS RM is a risk analysis and management methodology developed by the French National Cybersecurity Agency (ANSSI). It is a reference framework used to assess information security risks and develop risk treatment plans.

EBIOS RM is based on a structured, iterative methodology for analyzing risks. It includes several key steps, such as identifying assets, characterizing threats, assessing vulnerabilities, estimating impacts, and determining risk levels.

The EBIOS RM approach is distinguished by its use of risk scenarios, which simulate concrete situations and assess potential consequences for information security. These scenarios help provide a better understanding of risks and make informed decisions to mitigate them.

EBIOS RM also proposes security measures and risk treatment actions, allowing organizations to establish action plans to reduce identified risks. It encourages considering constraints, issues, and objectives specific to the organization to adapt risk management to its unique context.

Widely used in France, particularly in the public and private sectors, EBIOS RM provides a structured and comprehensive approach to risk management, enabling organizations to make informed decisions and strengthen their security posture.

EBIOS RM follows a seven-step approach to risk analysis and management. Here is an overview of the main steps, actions to take, and associated deliverables:

a) **Initialization Step**:
- **Actions**: Start the project, designate key actors, define objectives.
- **Deliverables**: Project charter, risk management plan, list of involved actors.

b) **Context Step:**
- **Actions**: Identify the study perimeter, assets to protect, stakeholders.
- **Deliverables**: Asset mapping, stakeholder identification, study perimeter definition.

c) **Risk Analysis Step:**
- **Actions**: Identify threats, vulnerabilities, estimate impacts.
- **Deliverables**: Risk matrix, threat list, vulnerability list, impact assessment.

d) **Risk Treatment Step:**
- **Actions**: Define security measures, develop risk treatment plans.
- **Deliverables**: Risk treatment plan, corrective action

plan, recommended security measures.

e) **Measure Selection Step**:
- **Actions**: Evaluate proposed security measures, select best options.
- **Deliverables**: Security measures analysis, selected measures.

f) **Implementation Step**:
- **Actions**: Implement security measures, track deployment.
- **Deliverables**: Implementation report, security measures deployment tracking.

g) **Risk Monitoring and Management Step**:
- **Actions**: Regularly evaluate security measures effectiveness, update preventive actions.
- **Deliverables**: Monitoring reports, updated risk management plan.

These steps take place in an iterative process, meaning it may be necessary to revisit and revise certain steps as new information or changes arise.

Note: Deliverables may vary depending on the specific context of the organization, the complexity of the risks, and regulatory requirements. It is recommended to refer to the official EBIOS RM documentation for detailed information on each step and corresponding deliverables.

C. Identification of Assets and Their Value

Identifying assets and their value is a fundamental step in establishing an Information Security Management System (ISMS). This process allows an organization to recognize the key assets comprising its information system, understand their importance, and better grasp the risks to which these assets are exposed. Here's how to identify assets and assess their value:

- **Asset Inventory**: Start by cataloging all the organization's assets, whether physical, logical, or human. Physical assets include IT or information equipment, premises, vehicles, etc. Logical assets cover IT systems, data, access management, software, applications, and more. Human assets pertain to the skills, knowledge, and sensitive information held by staff.
- **Asset Classification**: Once inventoried, assets should be classified by their importance, sensitivity, and value to the organization. This classification helps prioritize assets in terms of protection and establish appropriate security measures. For instance, customer personal data or trade secrets may be classified as highly sensitive assets, while office equipment might be considered of lesser importance.
- **Asset Value Assessment**: Assessing asset value involves several factors. These can include the financial value of assets, such as acquisition cost or market value, the operational value, reflecting the asset's contribution to organizational operations, and the strategic value, such as its impact on reputation or importance to achieving objectives.
- **Asset and Value Documentation**: It is essential to document identified assets, their classification, and their value. This creates a clear, up-to-date asset register, facilitates communication and understanding among stakeholders, and guides decisions regarding asset protection.

Note: Identifying assets and their value should involve the appropriate stakeholders, including managers from various departments and individuals with pertinent information. A collaborative approach ensures a comprehensive and accurate view of the organization's assets.

In summary, identifying assets and their value is a critical step for information security management. It allows an organization to understand its assets' significance, classify assets based on their sensitivity and value, and implement appropriate security measures for protection.

Tools, Tools, and More Tools

Several common tools are used for identifying assets within information security management. Here are some of the most popular:

- **Physical and Software Inventories**: These inventories help track hardware (equipment, devices, premises) and software assets (operating systems, applications, databases) within the organization. These tools may be dedicated IT solutions or asset management systems.
- **Questionnaires and Surveys**: These are effective tools for gathering information about assets from organizational stakeholders. They can be used to interview managers in each department to identify specific assets under their control.
- **Interviews and Individual Meetings**: Individual interviews with department heads or key information holders can be beneficial for obtaining details about assets and their importance. These interviews provide valuable insights into assets that might not be evident through other methods.
- **Document Analysis**: Reviewing existing documents, such as business plans, internal policies, financial reports, and other relevant materials, can help identify assets and understand their importance. This can be done by carefully examining these documents for asset-related information, classifications, and values.
- **Network Discovery and Monitoring Tools**: For IT assets, network discovery and monitoring tools can be used to automatically identify assets on the organization's network. These tools scan the network to detect systems,

devices, and active applications, providing a comprehensive view of IT assets.

Note: The choice of tools depends on the organization's specific needs, size, available resources, and the complexity of its information system. Some tools may be better suited for large organizations with advanced IT resources, while others may be more appropriate for smaller organizations with limited resources.

Using a combination of multiple tools and approaches is often the best solution for comprehensively identifying an organization's assets. It is also essential to keep asset information updated and regularly reviewed to reflect organizational and technological changes.

It's necessary to cross-check the information obtained, whether from physical inventories, questionnaires, interviews, or document analysis. Cross-referencing data from different sources provides a completer and more accurate picture of the organization's assets. For instance, information gathered from individual interviews can complement that obtained from a physical inventory or document analysis.

Cross-referencing these data ensures consistency, helps identify discrepancies or omissions, and provides a more reliable and thorough view of the organization's assets. This process ensures all relevant information is considered in identifying, classifying, and evaluating assets, thereby enhancing the accuracy and reliability of the information that forms the foundation of information security management.

D. Risk Analysis and Evaluation

Risk analysis and evaluation are essential steps for information security. These processes allow organizations to identify the risks they face, assess their severity and probability, and make informed decisions about implementing appropriate risk treatment measures. Here's how to conduct an effective risk analysis and evaluation:

- **Risk Identification**: Begin by identifying the risks your organization is exposed to. This involves listing threats, existing vulnerabilities, and assets that may be affected. Threats may include cyberattacks, natural disasters, human errors, etc. Vulnerabilities may be gaps in security systems, operational weaknesses, or defective processes. Identify critical assets, such as sensitive data, essential infrastructure, and strategic information.

- **Impact Estimation**: Assess the potential consequences of identified risks on the organization's assets. This may include financial, operational, legal, regulatory, or reputational impacts. Quantify these impacts as much as possible in terms of financial costs, recovery time, productivity loss, etc. The greater the impact, the more concerning the risk for the organization.

- **Probability Evaluation**: Estimate the likelihood of identified risks occurring. This can be done using historical data, statistics, internal or external expertise, or scenario analyses. Probability can be expressed in terms of frequency (e.g., rare, occasional, frequent) or percentage. It is essential to base probability assessments on reliable and relevant information.

- **Risk Level Assessment**: Once impacts and probabilities have been estimated, risk levels can be determined. This can be done using a risk matrix, with impacts represented on one axis and probabilities on the other. Risk levels can be categorized, for example, as high, medium, or low, or using numerical scores. This helps prioritize risks by focusing on those with the highest levels.

- **Selecting Treatment Measures**: After evaluating risks, it is necessary to determine the appropriate treatment measures. This may include risk acceptance, implementing preventive or protective measures, transferring the risk to a third party (e.g., insurance), or avoiding the risk by discontinuing certain activities or technologies. Treatment measures should be proportional to the risk level and aligned with the organization's objectives and resources.

Note: Risk analysis and evaluation are ongoing, evolving processes. Risks and environments change over time, necessitating regular monitoring and adjustments to treatment measures. Involving stakeholders, fostering collaboration across organizational departments, and ensuring transparent communication are also essential elements of effective risk analysis and evaluation.

Key Success Factors

By following these tips, you'll be able to conduct a more effective risk analysis and evaluation, making well-informed decisions to protect your organization against threats and vulnerabilities.

- **Involve Stakeholders**: It is essential to involve key stakeholders in the risk analysis and evaluation process. This may include representatives from various departments, information security experts, operational managers, and external parties such as auditors or consultants. Their expertise and perspectives will contribute to a more comprehensive risk analysis.
- **Collect Reliable Data**: Accurate risk evaluation relies on gathering reliable and relevant data. This may include historical data on past incidents, information on emerging threats, industry statistics, or case studies. Fact-based data strengthens the credibility of risk analysis.
- **Use Appropriate Methods and Tools**: Select risk analysis methods and tools best suited to your organization. These may include qualitative, quantitative, or hybrid methods, depending on risk complexity and available resources. Also, use suitable tools like risk matrices, specialized software, or spreadsheets to

facilitate analysis and documentation.

- **Be Realistic and Pragmatic**: When evaluating risks, ensure you are realistic and pragmatic in estimating impacts and probabilities. Avoid speculation or exaggeration and rely on tangible data to assess risks. An objective and balanced evaluation supports fact-based decision-making.

- **Prioritize Risks**: Once risks are evaluated, prioritize them based on their severity and probability. This allows focusing efforts on the most critical and urgent risks. Use clear and established prioritization criteria, such as financial, operational, or regulatory impacts, to rank risks.

- **Communicate Effectively**: Communication is essential during risk analysis and evaluation. Ensure that you clearly convey analysis results, risk levels, and recommended treatment measures. Involve appropriate stakeholders in decision-making and ensure information is understood and accepted by all.

- **Regularly Reevaluate**: Risks evolve over time, so it is important to regularly reassess risk analysis and evaluation. Schedule periodic reviews to account for new risks, organizational changes, technological advances, or shifts in the information security landscape. Risk management is an ongoing and iterative process.

5. STEP 3: BUILD THE ISMS

A. Defining Information Security Objectives

What is a security objective?

A security objective is a specific goal or target related to protecting an organization's assets, data, and processes from security threats and risks. It represents what the organization aims to achieve regarding information security and is a key component in maintaining business continuity.

Security objectives are typically formulated to address the specific needs and requirements of the organization. They may be defined based on applicable laws and regulations, contractual obligations, industry best practices, or the organization's internal policies. Often, they incorporate a blend of multiple requirements.

Measurable security objectives are critical as they make it easier to assess progress, track performance, and determine if objectives have been met.

There are several reasons why having measurable objectives is beneficial.

Firstly, measurable objectives provide a clear framework for assessing progress in information security. Establishing concrete measures makes it easier to determine whether the organization is on track to meet its security objectives. Regular assessments also allow for monitoring efforts and making necessary adjustments.

Moreover, measurable objectives facilitate the tracking of an organization's security performance. Using objective measures, it is possible to compare results with the set goals and identify areas that need improvement. This performance evaluation helps pinpoint areas for corrective action and focuses resources on the most critical aspects.

Measurable objectives also play a key role in data-driven decision-making. They provide solid benchmarks to guide security-related decisions, helping to avoid decisions based on emotions and gut feelings. By relying on clear metrics, it becomes easier to prioritize resources and actions to achieve established security objectives, enabling informed choices and focused efforts on the most important aspects.

Furthermore, measurable objectives enhance accountability within the organization. Each stakeholder can be held accountable for contributing to achieving security objectives. Objective measures provide a basis for evaluating individual and collective performance, fostering a culture of continuous improvement. This shared responsibility strengthens commitment to security objectives.

Finally, measurable objectives aid in communication and transparency around the efforts required. Metrics offer a common language for discussing progress, challenges, and results. This promotes mutual understanding among stakeholders and facilitates communication with management, security teams, and relevant external parties. Transparency in communication builds trust and enhances collaboration among the various stakeholders.

In sum, measurable security objectives offer numerous advantages for managing information security. They allow for objective assessment of progress, performance tracking, informed decision-making, clear accountability, and transparent communication. By setting measurable objectives, an organization can focus on achieving concrete results and continuously improving its security posture.

Examples of Security Objectives

Here are some of the most common examples of security objectives:

- **Confidentiality**: Protect sensitive and confidential information from unauthorized access or disclosure. Example objective: Implement access control and encryption mechanisms to ensure data confidentiality.
- **Integrity**: Ensure the accuracy, integrity, and reliability of information by preventing unauthorized modification or alteration. Example objective: Implement change control mechanisms to ensure only authorized individuals can modify data.
- **Availability**: Ensure that systems, services, and information are available as needed by the organization, preventing unplanned interruptions. Example objective: Set up backup and redundancy mechanisms to ensure continuous availability of critical systems.
- **Authentication**: Verify the identity of users and entities to ensure that only authorized individuals have access to resources and information. Example objective: Implement strong authentication, such as complex passwords and biometric or multi-factor methods, to enhance system access security.
- **Traceability**: Establish a clear and complete audit trail to track actions taken on systems and data, enabling quick detection and response to security incidents. Example objective: Set up activity logs and monitoring tools to record and analyze system events.
- **Regulatory Compliance**: Meet legal, regulatory, and

contractual information security requirements. Example objective: Ensure information security policies and procedures comply with applicable laws and regulations, such as GDPR or PCI DSS.

These examples illustrate some of the many possible security objectives. Each organization should identify its security objectives based on its specific needs, activities, and priorities. These objectives will form the foundation for establishing a solid information security framework and defining appropriate control measures.

How to Define Security Objectives

Defining security objectives is a sensitive process that requires a thoughtful, strategic approach. Here are steps for effectively setting security objectives:

1. **Needs Analysis**: Start by analyzing your organization's specific information security needs. This may include identifying critical assets, sensitive business processes, applicable regulations, contractual requirements, and specific risks your organization faces. Understand the unique security issues and priorities for your organization.

2. **Alignment with the Organization's Overall Strategy**: Security objectives must align with the organization's overall strategy. Identify your company's strategic objectives and core values, and ensure the security objectives support these key elements. Information security should be considered an enabler of the organization's overall strategy.

3. **Define Specific Objectives**: Once you clearly understand needs and overall strategy, define specific security objectives. Objectives should be clear, measurable, achievable, relevant, and time-bound (SMART). They should focus on concrete results and align with the previously identified security issues.

4. **Prioritize Objectives**: Consider available resources, the urgency of risks, and potential impacts to prioritize

security objectives. Ranking objectives based on their strategic importance and criticality to the organization may be helpful. This allows focusing efforts and resources on the most critical objectives.

5. **Involve Stakeholders**: Involve the appropriate stakeholders in defining security objectives, including company management, operational managers, security teams, regulatory compliance experts, and other key stakeholders. Their input and perspective are essential to setting realistic, relevant objectives.

6. **Establish Monitoring Measures**: For each security objective, define specific metrics to evaluate progress and performance. These metrics may be quantitative or qualitative, depending on the objective's nature. Be sure to choose relevant indicators that reflect the achievement of objectives and allow measurement of results.

7. **Regularly Reevaluate and Adjust**: Security objectives are not static and should be reevaluated and adjusted regularly. Take into account internal and external changes that could impact security objectives, such as evolving threats, technologies, or regulations. Conduct periodic reviews to ensure objectives remain relevant and make necessary adjustments as needed.

Note: By following these steps, you will be able to define clear security objectives aligned with your organization's overall strategy and suited to your specific environment's needs.

Security KPIs

A KPI (Key Performance Indicator) is a key metric used to measure and evaluate progress against predefined objectives. In information security, KPIs are essential metrics that allow for monitoring and quantifying an organization's security performance. They provide an overview of results achieved and the effectiveness of security measures implemented.

There are several KPIs commonly used by information

security professionals, tailored to different sectors and specific goals. Here are some of the most common KPIs:

- **Security Incident Rate**: Measures the frequency of security incidents, such as data breaches, intrusion attempts, successful attacks, etc. A high incident rate may indicate vulnerabilities or weaknesses in security measures.

- **Mean Time to Detect (MTTD)**: Measures the average time required to detect an intrusion or security incident. A short MTTD is generally preferable as it enables faster response and potential reduction of damage.

- **Mean Time to Repair (MTTR)**: Measures the average time needed to resolve and remediate a security incident. A short MTTR indicates a fast response capability and minimizes the impact of incidents.

- **Compliance Rate**: Assesses the organization's level of compliance with specific security regulations, standards, or policies. A high compliance rate is typically an indicator of robust security measures.

- **Penetration Test Success Rate (Technical Audits)**: Measures the success rate of penetration tests conducted to assess system vulnerability. A high success rate may indicate security gaps that require further attention.

- **Security Awareness Rate**: Evaluates employees' level of awareness of information security through training, quizzes, or awareness campaigns. A high awareness rate is a positive indicator of the organization's security culture.

- **Patching Rate**: Measures the speed at which security patches are applied to systems and software to remediate known vulnerabilities. A high patching rate is needed for reducing the risk of exploiting known vulnerabilities.

- **False Alarm and False Positive Rate**: Assesses the accuracy of intrusion detection systems or monitoring tools. A low false alarm rate is desirable to minimize false positives and focus resources on real threats.

Note: It's essential to choose KPIs based on the organization's specific security objectives and priority areas. KPIs should be relevant, measurable, and aligned with the security issues identified in risk analyses. They should be regularly monitored and evaluated to make necessary adjustments and correspond to continuous improvement needs defined in the ISMS objectives.

In summary, KPIs play an essential role in monitoring and measuring security performance, enabling organizations to make informed decisions and demonstrate the effectiveness of their security efforts.

B. Drafting the General Information Security Policy

About Policies

An information security policy is a document that outlines the general directions, objectives, and guiding principles regarding security within an organization. The information security policy defines the broad guidelines and responsibilities related to protecting the organization's assets, data, and processes from security threats and risks.

The security policy is a fundamental component of information security governance. It provides a comprehensive and consistent framework to guide decisions and establish action plans for security within the organization. It should align with the organization's overall strategy and consider the specific security objectives defined previously (see previous point).

An effective security policy includes clear, precise, achievable, and measurable objectives. These objectives represent the specific results the organization aims to achieve in information security and must directly relate to the issues identified in risk analyses, as well as the selected KPIs for evaluating security performance.

The security policy should also include guiding principles. These principles provide foundational orientations and values that guide actions and decisions regarding information security. They form the ethical and strategic basis for defining appropriate security measures. Principles may include concepts like confidentiality, integrity, availability, accountability, compliance, and security awareness.

Note: The security policy should not be a static document but an evolving one. It must be regularly reviewed and updated to adapt to changes in the security environment, new risks, and technological advancements. A well-crafted, regularly updated security policy allows for a strong defensive posture, ensuring objectives and principles remain relevant.

The security policy also serves as an essential tool for communicating and raising awareness among employees and stakeholders about security issues and best practices. It fosters a culture of security within the organization by setting clear expectations and encouraging compliance with defined security measures.

In brief, the information security policy establishes objectives and guiding principles to direct actions and decisions related to security within an organization. It provides a strategic and ethical framework for implementing appropriate security measures. As an evolving document, it must be regularly reviewed to reflect changes in the security environment and maintain a robust security posture.

Defining the General Information Security Policy

Defining the General Information Security Policy (GISP) is a critical step in managing information security within an organization. Here are the key steps for creating an effective GISP:

a) **Needs Analysis**: Start by analyzing your organization's specific needs for information system security. Identify critical assets, data, and processes, as well as the risks and threats they face. Understand the regulatory, contractual, and internal requirements related to information security.

b) **Management Commitment**: Obtain active commitment and support from the organization's management. Information security must be treated as a strategic priority, with high-level support to ensure effective implementation of the GISP.

c) **Defining Objectives**: Establish clear, measurable objectives for information system security. Objectives should align with the organization's needs and identified security issues. They should be specific, achievable, and relevant to ensure clear direction and guide actions and decisions. Remember, the more measurable they are, the more manageable they become.

d) **Defining Guiding Principles**: Identify the guiding principles that will serve as the ethical and strategic foundation of the GISP. These principles may include confidentiality, integrity, availability, accountability, compliance, and security awareness. They should align with the values and culture of the organization.

e) **Developing the Control Framework**: Define the framework of control measures needed to achieve security objectives. This may include policies, procedures, standards, guidelines, and best practices for information system security. The control framework should be tailored to the organization's needs and based on standards such as ISO 27001.

f) **Communication and Awareness**: Ensure that the

GISP is effectively communicated to all employees and relevant stakeholders. Organize security awareness sessions to inform users of policies, procedures, and best practices to follow. Regular communication and awareness are essential for promoting a security culture and encouraging compliance.

g) **Implementation and Monitoring**: Implement the defined control measures within the GISP and ensure their effectiveness. Conduct regular audits and assessments to evaluate compliance and the effectiveness of security measures. Periodically review and update the GISP to reflect changes in the security environment and the organization's needs.

By following these steps, you can define a solid General Information Security Policy aligned with your organization's needs, providing clear direction for managing information system security.

What the GISP Should Contain

A General Information Security Policy (GISP) should contain several key elements to be valid and effective. Here are the essential components of a GISP, along with examples and advice:

a) **Introduction**: An engaging introduction explaining the importance of information system security and the organization's commitment to protecting its assets and data.
   - *Example*: "This General Information Security Policy (GISP) aims to ensure the confidentiality, integrity, and availability of our information systems and prevent security incidents. It reflects our commitment to protecting our assets and maintaining the trust of our customers, partners, and stakeholders."
   - *Advice*: Use clear and concise language to

effectively communicate security objectives and principles.

b) **Security Objectives**: Specific objectives the organization aims to achieve in information system security. Objectives should be measurable and aligned with the organization's needs and security challenges.

- o *Example*: "Ensure customer data confidentiality by implementing appropriate encryption measures." "Reduce intrusion risks by strengthening access controls and strong authentication."
- o *Advice*: Define realistic and achievable objectives, considering available resources and operational constraints.

c) **Guiding Principles**: The fundamental principles that guide actions and decisions in information system security. These principles serve as the ethical and strategic foundation for defining appropriate security measures.

- o *Example*: "Confidentiality: We are committed to protecting the confidentiality of sensitive customer information by implementing appropriate access controls and access rights management policies." "Accountability: Each employee is responsible for information system security and must adhere to established security policies and procedures."
- o *Advice*: The guiding principles should reflect the organization's values and culture and comply with applicable standards and regulations.

d) **Control Framework**: The policies, procedures, standards, and guidelines to be implemented for information system security. This control framework should be tailored to the organization's needs and based on best security practices.

- o *Example*: An example of a control framework in

an ISMS is establishing an identity management framework. This framework can include specific policies, procedures, and guidelines for managing user identities and controlling access to sensitive systems and information. It may involve measures such as assigning unique identifiers to each user, managing access rights based on user needs and roles, conducting regular access rights reviews, and implementing authentication and identity validation controls.

o *Advice*: When developing the identity management framework, it's essential to understand the organization's specific needs regarding access to sensitive information and identity control. Adopting best practices, such as Identity and Access Management (IAM), and aligning with recognized standards like ISO 27001 is crucial. Implementing regular access rights reviews ensures users only have the privileges necessary for their professional activities. Lastly, user awareness and training on identity management best practices are vital for secure and responsible use of systems and information.

e) **Responsibilities**: The roles and responsibilities assigned to various stakeholders for implementing and adhering to the GISP, including management, managers, employees, and security teams.

o *Example*: "Management is responsible for providing resources for implementing security measures and promoting a security culture within the organization." "Managers are responsible for ensuring their teams adhere to established security policies and procedures."

o *Advice*: Clarify the responsibilities of each stakeholder and ensure expectations are clearly communicated.

f) **Training and Awareness**: Initiatives for security training and awareness to inform employees about policies, procedures, and best security practices.

- o *Example*: "Mandatory training sessions will be organized for all employees to raise awareness of security risks and inform them of best practices." "Regular awareness campaigns will be launched to maintain a dynamic security culture and encourage responsible behaviors."
- o *Advice*: Use various communication methods, such as in-person training, information documents, emails, and posters, to reach employees effectively.

g) **Review and Update**: The frequency with which the GISP will be reviewed and updated to reflect changes in the security environment and organizational needs.

- o *Example*: "The GISP will be reviewed annually by the information security team to ensure relevance and effectiveness. Additional reviews will occur if significant changes in risks or regulations arise."
- o *Advice*: Establish a formal process for reviewing and approving the GISP to ensure regular updates.

By following these examples and tips, you will be able to create a comprehensive General Information Security Policy suited to your organization's needs. Remember to consider your environment's specific characteristics and consult key stakeholders to gain their feedback and support in defining the GISP.

C. Additional Security Policies

The General Information Security Policy (GISP) provides the overall strategic framework for information security within an organization. However, it is not the only security policy needed. Various specific aspects of information security require detailed policies derived from the GISP, focusing on specific domains. These subsidiary policies should be drafted based on the objectives defined in the GISP and set forth appropriate security principles and rules.

Subsidiary security policies are documents detailing specific security measures for areas such as access management, data protection, incident management, information backup, etc. Each of these policies must align with the security objectives established in the GISP and provide clear, detailed guidance for associated security practices and procedures.

When drafting these policies, it's essential to define specific security principles that reflect the organization's values and support its overall security objectives. These principles may cover aspects such as confidentiality, integrity, availability, traceability, regulatory compliance, risk management, etc. Security principles should be tailored to the needs of the area covered by each subsidiary policy.

For example, an access management policy might outline the procedures for assigning access rights to systems and data, based on the principle of confidentiality, ensuring that only authorized individuals can access sensitive information. A data protection policy may establish specific rules for encryption, classification, and secure data disposal, based on the principle of integrity, ensuring that information is protected against unauthorized alteration.

Each sector-specific policy should be written clearly and understandably, using language appropriate for the stakeholders involved. The responsibilities of different actors involved in enforcing the policy should be specified, as well as the procedures to follow and the control measures to implement. It is also important to establish monitoring and evaluation mechanisms to verify compliance and ensure ongoing effectiveness.

In summary, the GISP forms the strategic framework for information security, but this general policy must be complemented by subsidiary security policies addressing specific areas. These policies should be based on security objectives and establish principles adapted to each area. They provide detailed guidance for implementing specific security measures and should be regularly reviewed to stay relevant and effective.

The Ideal "Set"

There is no universal "ideal" set of security policies, as security needs and requirements vary from one organization to another. However, it is possible to identify a set of commonly recommended security policies to cover the essential aspects of information security. Here are examples of security policies frequently implemented:

a) **Access Management Policy**: Defines rules for granting and revoking access rights to systems and sensitive data. It specifies requirements for strong authentication, role-based access control, and privilege management.

b) **Data Classification Policy**: Establishes rules for classifying data according to its sensitivity and impact on the organization. It defines classification levels, data labeling procedures, and appropriate protection measures for each category.

c) **Change Management Policy**: Outlines measures and rules for managing changes within the organization's systems and infrastructures. It specifies steps for planning, risk assessment, testing, and validating changes before deployment.

d) **Incident Management Policy**: Establishes rules for detecting, managing, and responding to security incidents. It defines the responsibilities of response teams, reporting channels, and steps for notification, investigation, and remediation.

e) **Vulnerability Management Policy**: Defines rules for identifying, assessing, and managing vulnerabilities in systems and applications. It specifies scanning frequencies, criticality levels, remediation timeframes, and corrective actions.

f) **Password Management Policy**: Sets rules for the creation, use, and management of passwords. It defines complexity requirements, periodic renewal, non-reuse, and secure password storage.

g) **Data Backup and Restoration Policy**: Describes rules and measures for regularly backing up critical data, secure storage measures, and periodic restoration tests to ensure data availability in case of disaster.

h) **Vendor Management Policy**: Establishes criteria for selecting, evaluating, and managing external vendors and partners. It specifies security requirements, contractual clauses, and monitoring measures to ensure the security of shared information.

i) **Mobile Device Management Policy**: Defines rules for secure use of mobile devices, such as smartphones and tablets. It specifies encryption, access control, app management, and data wiping requirements in case of loss or theft.

j) **Removable Media Management Policy**: Sets rules for using removable media, such as USB drives and external hard drives. It defines encryption, antivirus scanning, and access control requirements to prevent data leaks.

k) **Physical Security Incident Management Policy**: Describes rules for managing physical security incidents, such as intrusions, theft, or material damage. It specifies alert, response, and communication steps in case of a physical incident.

l) **Security Awareness Policy**: Establishes security awareness initiatives to inform and train employees on security risks, best practices, and safe behaviors. It may include training programs, awareness campaigns, and regular security reminders.

Guidelines for Policy Writing

Nothing is worse than a security policy with outdated objectives and impractical principles. Below is a list of tips to avoid common pitfalls.

- **Understand Your Organization's Needs**: Before drafting a security policy, understand the specific information security needs of your organization. Identify relevant assets, risks, and security issues.
- **Be Clear and Concise**: Use clear, understandable language to effectively communicate security directives. Avoid technical jargon or ambiguous wording that could confuse or discourage stakeholders.
- **Take an Objective-Based Approach**: Define clear, measurable objectives for each security policy. Objectives should align with the organization's needs and provide direction for implementing security measures.
- **Define Security Principles**: Articulate clear security principles to serve as the ethical and strategic foundation for your policies. Principles should match the organization's values and culture.
- **Involve Stakeholders**: Consult key stakeholders, including security experts, managers, and employees, when drafting policies. Their input and support are essential for ensuring policy adoption and effectiveness.
- **Avoid Excessive Technical Details**: Security policies should not be overloaded with technical details. Focus on objectives, principles, and general security measures

rather than specific technicalities, which can quickly become outdated.

- **Reference Standards and Regulations**: Ensure your policies comply with applicable standards and regulations, such as ISO 27001, NIST, or data protection laws. Include references to relevant documents for easier compliance.

- **Consider Best Practices**: Refer to best practices in information security and recognized frameworks to ensure appropriate security measures are included.

- **Be Realistic and Achievable**: Security policies must be realistic and achievable given your organization's resources and constraints. Avoid imposing excessively restrictive or impractical measures.

- **Educate and Raise Awareness**: Remember that security policies must be understood and followed by employees. Plan training and awareness initiatives to inform users about policies, procedures, and best practices.

- **Review Regularly**: Security policies should be reviewed and updated regularly to reflect changes in the security environment, technologies, and organizational needs.

- **Involve Management**: Obtain active commitment and support from the organization's management. Information security is an organizational responsibility, and management's involvement is essential to ensure the implementation and adherence to security policies.

By following these guidelines, organizations can develop effective and up-to-date security policies that are clear, achievable, and supported across all levels.

D. D. Communication Plan

The communication plan is another essential element in implementing security policies. It aims to inform and raise awareness among relevant stakeholders about policies, procedures, and best practices in information security. Here's how to define an effective communication plan:

a) **Identify Stakeholders**: Identify the different stakeholders impacted by security policies, including employees, managers, executives, suppliers, and external partners.

b) **Analyze Communication Needs**: Determine the key information each stakeholder group needs to understand and comply with security policies. Also, identify the most appropriate communication channels for effectively reaching each target group.

c) **Establish Communication Objectives**: Define specific objectives for your communication plan, such as increasing security awareness, ensuring understanding of policies and procedures, and fostering active stakeholder engagement.

d) **Develop Key Messages**: Identify the main messages you wish to convey to each target group. These messages should be clear, concise, and tailored to the audience.

e) **Select Communication Channels**: Choose the most appropriate communication channels for each target group. This could include information meetings, training sessions, emails, notices, videos, internal newsletters, intranet postings, or online collaboration platforms.

f) **Plan Communication Activities**: Establish a detailed schedule of communication activities, outlining dates, responsible parties, content, and channels for each activity.

g) **Create Communication Materials**: Develop attractive, clear materials to convey key messages. These could include PowerPoint presentations, fact sheets, practical guides, explainer videos, or infographics.

h) **Engage Stakeholders**: Encourage active engagement by involving stakeholders in the communication process. Seek their feedback, answer questions, and promote participation in training sessions or workshops.

i) **Evaluate Communication Effectiveness**: Regularly evaluate the effectiveness of your communication plan. Use surveys, questionnaires, or monitoring indicators to gather stakeholder feedback and adjust communication activities as needed.

j) **Review and Update**: Regularly review and update your communication plan to ensure it remains relevant and aligned with the evolving needs of your organization.

Note: By creating a structured, tailored communication plan, you can ensure that security policies are conveyed in a clear, understandable, and engaging manner, thereby fostering a proactive security culture within your organization.

What Should the Communication Plan Include?

Creating a formal document called a "communication plan" for security policies is recommended. This document details the strategies, objectives, and planned communication activities to promote security policies within the organization. It's essential for this communication plan to be validated by key stakeholders, including senior management, HR managers, and operational management.

Validation from these stakeholders is important for several reasons:

- **Management Commitment**: Management validation confirms their commitment to security policies and emphasizes the importance of communication in policy implementation, giving legitimacy and authority to the communication plan.

- **HR Involvement**: HR managers play a central role in internal communication. Their validation ensures that the communication plan aligns with existing HR policies and practices and addresses employees' specific needs for awareness and training.
- **Support from Operational Management**: Validation from operational managers ensures the plan is realistic, achievable, and tailored to the needs of various business units. Their support helps facilitate the implementation and adherence of employees to security policies.

Obtaining validation of the communication plan from these stakeholders should precede its implementation. This can be done through meetings, presentations, or formal proposal documents. Gathering their feedback, suggestions, and support is vital to ensuring the plan meets the organization's overall expectations and needs.

Once validated, the communication plan should be widely shared and communicated to all involved in implementing security policies. It should be treated as a key reference document to guide communication activities and ensure consistent messaging on security.

By involving HR, management, and other stakeholders in the validation of the communication plan, you can secure strong support and a shared understanding of the objectives and communication activities. This fosters the adoption and adherence to security policies within your organization.

A communication plan for security policies should include the following elements:

a) **Communication Objectives**: Clearly define the specific objectives you want to achieve with your communication plan. This might include goals such as raising awareness about the importance of information security, informing stakeholders about security policies and procedures, promoting best practices, etc.

b) **Target Stakeholders**: Identify the different stakeholders affected by security policies. This could include employees, managers, senior management, suppliers, external partners, etc.

c) **Key Messages**: Identify the key messages you want to convey to each target group. These messages should be clear, concise, and tailored to the specific concerns and needs of each group.

d) **Communication Channels**: Select the most appropriate channels to effectively reach each target group. This may include information meetings, training sessions, emails, notices, internal newsletters, intranet posts, online collaboration platforms, etc.

e) **Activity Schedule**: Develop a detailed schedule of communication activities, setting dates, responsible parties, content, and channels for each activity.

f) **Communication Materials**: Create attractive, clear materials to convey key messages. These may include PowerPoint presentations, fact sheets, practical guides, explainer videos, infographics, etc.

g) **Stakeholder Engagement**: Encourage active engagement from stakeholders by involving them in the communication process. This could involve gathering their feedback, answering their questions, promoting participation in training sessions or workshops, etc.

h) **Effectiveness Evaluation**: Plan evaluation mechanisms to measure the effectiveness of your communication plan. Use surveys, questionnaires, or monitoring indicators to gather stakeholder feedback and assess the impact of your communication activities.

i) **Review and Update**: Regularly review and update your

communication plan to ensure it remains relevant and aligned with the changing needs of your organization.

By including these elements in your communication plan, you can ensure effective and consistent dissemination of security policies within your organization, while encouraging stakeholder engagement and compliance with security practices.

Which KPIs to Implement?

When measuring the effectiveness of a communication plan for security policies, it's helpful to define relevant key performance indicators (KPIs). Here are some examples of KPIs to consider:

- **Awareness Rate**: Measure stakeholder awareness of security policies through surveys, questionnaires, or knowledge tests. This can give an indication of the overall understanding of security policies and practices.
- **Policy Adoption Rate**: Track the percentage of employees who have signed and acknowledged security policies. This can reflect employees' commitment to and willingness to comply with policies.
- **Number of Training Sessions or Workshops**: Count the number of training sessions or workshops organized as part of the communication plan. This can help gauge employee engagement in awareness-raising activities and the reach of training provided.
- **Participation Rate**: Measure the percentage of employees who participated in training sessions, workshops, or other communication activities. This can reflect employees' interest in learning about security policies.
- **Compliance Level**: Assess compliance with security policies by tracking reported non-compliance incidents or conducting internal audits. This can help evaluate communication effectiveness and highlight areas needing

improvement.

- **Incident Reporting Rate**: Measure the rate of security incident reporting by employees. A high rate may indicate increased security awareness and an encouraging reporting culture.
- **Reduction in Security Incidents**: Track the number and severity of security incidents before and after implementing the communication plan. A significant reduction in incidents may indicate improved understanding and adherence to security policies.
- **Stakeholder Feedback**: Gather feedback from stakeholders on the effectiveness of the communication plan and their overall satisfaction. This can help identify strengths and areas for improvement.

It's essential to set specific goals for each KPI, establish initial baseline measurements, and regularly monitor progress to evaluate results and make necessary adjustments to your communication plan.

E. Translating Policies into Procedures

Translating policies into procedures is an important step in implementing an effective information security management system. This process turns broad directives into concrete actions, ensuring a shared understanding of security measures, facilitating compliance, training, and change management. By following this approach, organizations can strengthen their security posture and reduce information security risks.

When it comes to effectively implementing information security policies within an organization, translating them into clear, actionable procedures is essential. This conversion allows general directives to be transformed into specific actions by providing detailed instructions on how to implement security measures.

Translating policies into procedures is important for several reasons. First, it ensures a unified understanding of security measures across the organization. By converting policies into detailed procedures, both managers and employees receive precise guidance on actions to take, processes to follow, and best practices to adopt. This prevents ambiguity and ensures consistent application of security measures.

Second, the translation facilitates the establishment of controls and necessary actions to ensure compliance with security policies. Procedures describe specific steps to follow to implement security measures, simplifying their application and monitoring. This also guarantees that policies are converted into tangible actions, enhancing the overall effectiveness of the information security management system.

Additionally, translating policies into procedures supports employee training and awareness. By providing detailed and practical instructions, procedures enable employees to clearly understand their responsibilities and the actions needed to ensure information security. This aids in training new employees and providing periodic reminders to current employees, reinforcing the organization's security culture.

Finally, translating policies into procedures also simplifies change management and business continuity. Detailed procedures help identify potential impacts of changes, foresee required security measures, and ensure that critical processes remain operational in case of incidents or disruptions.

Policy, Procedure, or Work Instructions?

In information security management, it is essential to understand the differences between policies, processes, procedures, and work instructions. While these terms are often used interchangeably, they refer to distinct elements of the information security management system (ISMS). Here's an explanation of each concept:

- **Policies**: Formal statements that establish the principles and objectives of information security within an organization. They provide overall direction on how the organization should address information security, outlining broad guidelines and expectations, and serve as a guiding framework for information security activities. Typically approved by management, policies are binding for all members of the organization.

- **Processes**: Coordinated sets of activities that transform inputs into desired results. Processes outline key steps, roles, responsibilities, workflows, and interactions needed to achieve a specific goal. In the context of information security, processes may include activities such as asset identification, risk assessment, incident management, and security awareness. Processes are generally more detailed than policies, offering guidance on accomplishing specific tasks.

- **Procedures**: Step-by-step detailed instructions describing how to complete a specific task within a process. Procedures offer precise guidance on actions, stakeholder responsibilities, and timelines to ensure consistent and effective execution of information security activities.

- **Work Instructions**: Even more detailed documents providing precise guidance on how to complete specific tasks within procedures. They outline exact steps, tools to use, standards to follow, and expected outcomes for each task stage. Work instructions are often used by operators or technicians to carry out specific tasks consistently and in line with security requirements.

Writing Procedures

Writing information security procedures is necessary for ensuring the consistent and effective implementation of security activities within an organization. Here are some tips for drafting clear and easily understood information security procedures:

a) **Identify Objectives**: Before drafting a procedure, it's essential to clearly understand its objective and what you aim to achieve. This may include specific actions related to information security, such as password management, data classification, data backup, etc.

b) **Define Steps**: A procedure should be logically organized, detailing the specific steps needed to complete the task. Divide the procedure into distinct sections, detailing each step sequentially.

c) **Use Clear and Concise Language**: Avoid complex technical terms and use straightforward language that all users can understand. Explain each step concisely and precisely, using action verbs to indicate what should be done.

d) **Include Examples and Illustrations**: To aid understanding, include concrete examples or visual aids to explain steps. This can help users visualize the process and understand how to apply the instructions.

e) **Mention Responsibilities**: Clearly indicate the responsibilities and roles of those involved in executing the procedure. This avoids any confusion regarding individual responsibilities and ensures consistent task execution.

f) **Provide References and Useful Links**: If needed, include references to documents, policies, standards, or external guidelines necessary to complete the procedure. This allows users to find additional information as needed.

g) **Test and Review**: Before finalizing a procedure, test it in a controlled environment to ensure its effectiveness. Gather feedback from users on the clarity and feasibility of steps and make necessary adjustments.

Reviewing Procedures

Regularly reviewing information security procedures is essential to maintain their relevance, effectiveness, and compliance with technological changes and organizational needs. Here's an overview of when to review procedures:

- **Regularly Scheduled Reviews**: Establish a regular schedule for reviewing information security procedures, whether annually, bi-annually, or according to significant changes in the security environment.
- **Organizational Changes**: When there are organizational changes, such as restructurings, mergers, or acquisitions, procedures should be reviewed to reflect new structures and responsibilities, ensuring alignment with current operational processes.
- **Technological Advancements**: Rapid technological developments may render existing procedures obsolete or necessitate modifications to ensure adequate information protection. Therefore, procedures should be reviewed to adapt to new technologies and incorporate security best practices.
- **Regulatory and Standards Updates**: Information security regulations and standards are constantly evolving. Procedures must be reviewed to ensure compliance with legal requirements and industry best practices.
- **Feedback and Security Incidents**: Security incidents, internal or external audits, and feedback can reveal gaps in existing procedures. Reviewing procedures then becomes necessary to correct weaknesses and strengthen security measures.
- **Stakeholder Involvement**: When reviewing procedures, it's essential to involve relevant stakeholders, such as

operational managers, security specialists, employee representatives, etc. Their contributions and feedback can enrich the review process and ensure a comprehensive approach.

During the procedure review, it's recommended to take a structured approach: examine each step, verify its relevance and effectiveness, update references, responsibilities, and security measures as needed, document changes, and ensure communication of new procedures to all concerned users.

6. STEP 4: IMPLEMENTING THE CONTROLS

A control is a specific measure implemented to mitigate risks related to information security. Controls are preventive, corrective, or protective actions aimed at reducing vulnerabilities and minimizing the impact and/or frequency of one or multiple risks on information assets.

A control can take the form of a policy, procedure, operational practice, technology, or a non-exhaustive combination of these elements. It is designed to establish rules, guidelines, or restrictions to prevent security incidents, detect breaches, or minimize the consequences of incidents.

On the other hand, a security measure refers to a specific action put in place to protect the organization's assets, ensuring the level of information security defined by the organization. Security measures are thus concrete, tangible means of applying controls and implementing appropriate security practices.

Security measures can include technical aspects such as data encryption, firewalls, effective identity and access management, data backup and restoration, system monitoring, etc. They can also cover organizational aspects, including user training and awareness, incident management, change management, physical protection of facilities, and third-party management (partners, clients, suppliers), among others.

By combining appropriate controls and security measures, an organization can establish a strong infrastructure for protecting its information assets. Controls define requirements and guidelines, while security measures translate these requirements into specific actions.

It is essential to note that controls and security measures must be tailored to the specific needs of each organization. They should be continually evaluated, tested, and updated to adapt to technological advancements, emerging threats, and organizational changes.

Implementing Effective Control Measures

Implementing effective control measures is an important step in managing information security. Once risks are accurately and methodically identified and assessed, concrete steps must be taken to mitigate these risks and protect the organization's information assets. This is where the "Implement Control Measures" phase comes in.

This step involves defining and implementing appropriate security controls to reduce identified vulnerabilities and minimize the potential impacts of risks on the information system. As previously mentioned, control measures can take various forms, such as policies, procedures, technologies, training, audits, and monitoring processes.

The primary goal of this phase is to ensure the protection of the organization's assets by implementing security measures tailored to its specific needs. This requires selecting appropriate controls based on identified risks, legal and regulatory requirements, industry best practices, and the organization's information security objectives. Referring to the previously defined ISMS scope can be helpful here, as it contains ISMS-related challenges and dependencies.

Establishing effective control measures requires a holistic approach that encompasses all relevant organizational aspects, including human resources, technology, processes, and external partners. Clearly defining responsibilities, developing detailed policies and procedures, implementing monitoring and control mechanisms, and providing continuous training and awareness for employees are all essential.

By implementing these control measures, an organization can strengthen its information security posture, reduce risks, and build stakeholder trust. A proactive, organization-specific approach is key to ensuring effective control measures and maintaining strong, resilient information security.

Certification Audit for an Information Security Management System (ISMS)

In a certification audit for an Information Security Management System (ISMS), there are generally two distinct stages: Stage 1 and Stage 2. Each stage has specific objectives and focuses on key aspects of the certification process.

- **Stage 1** focuses on evaluating the governance of the ISMS. The auditor examines the policies, procedures, roles, and responsibilities related to information security within the organization. The primary objective of this stage is to ensure that management has established strong governance in information security and that principles and objectives are clearly defined. The auditor also assesses whether the requirements of information security standards, such as ISO 27001, are considered in governance. Before the audit, it is possible to ask the auditor for the information they will need.
- **Stage 2** focuses on verifying the implementation of

security measures and controls defined within the ISMS. The auditor examines the implementation of policies and procedures and the effectiveness of established security measures. This may include assessments of risk management processes, access controls, incident management, security awareness, and other key aspects of information security. The primary objective of this stage is to confirm that control measures are adequate and effectively applied to protect the organization's information assets.

These two audit stages are mandatory and aim to assess the ISMS's compliance with defined standards. The audits validate that governance and security measures are in place, ensuring policies and procedures are followed and that controls are effective. Upon successful audit completion, the organization can achieve ISMS certification, attesting to its compliance with international information security standards.

It is essential to note that the certification audit is a rigorous process conducted by an accredited independent body. This process ensures an objective and impartial evaluation of the organization's ISMS, bolstering stakeholder trust and demonstrating a commitment to information security.

A. Selection and Implementation of Organizational Controls

Examples of Organizational Controls

Here are some common examples of organizational controls used to ensure information security:

- **Security Policies**: Establish formal policies that define principles, objectives, scope, and responsibilities in information security; examples include the general security policy and related policies like data classification, management policies, password policies, and access control policies.

- **Awareness and Training**: Provide regular information security awareness programs and training for all information system users to inform them of best practices, current threats, and risky behaviors to avoid.

- **Access Management**: Implement controls to manage and control access to information resources, such as using strong passwords, multi-factor authentication, access rights management, and privilege controls.

- **Third-Party Management**: Develop policies and procedures to evaluate, select, and monitor third parties with whom the organization shares sensitive information, including confidentiality agreements and security clauses.

- **Incident Management**: Develop security incident management plans to identify, report, manage, and mitigate security incidents, with clear procedures for notification, investigation, resolution, and prevention.

- **Change Management**: Set up control and approval processes to manage changes to the information system, infrastructure components like networks, and modifications to applications to avoid service interruptions, configuration errors, and vulnerabilities.

- **Physical Security**: Implement physical controls to protect facilities and infrastructure, such as restricted access to sensitive areas, surveillance systems, fire protection measures, and secure locking mechanisms.

- **Human Resources Management**: Adopt policies and procedures for employee selection, training, awareness, and management, including rigorous recruitment processes, background checks, confidentiality agreements, and security clauses in employment contracts.

- **Backup and Restoration Management**: Establish policies and procedures for regularly backing up critical data, testing data recovery, and ensuring backup availability as needed.

- **Monitoring and Auditing**: Implement continuous

monitoring, periodic reviews, and internal audits to assess control effectiveness, detect security anomalies, and ensure compliance with security policies and standards.

How to Choose Organizational Controls

The selection of appropriate organizational controls depends on several factors, including the specific risks the organization faces, the size and nature of its IT operations, legal and regulatory requirements, and best practices in the industry. Here are some steps to guide the process:

a) **Risk Assessment**: Begin with a comprehensive risk assessment related to information security within your organization. Identify vulnerabilities, threats, and potential impacts on information assets. This assessment will help pinpoint areas where controls are necessary.

b) **Regulatory Compliance**: Identify applicable laws, regulations, and standards for your industry. Ensure that your organizational controls comply with these requirements.

c) **Industry Best Practices**: Familiarize yourself with recommended information security best practices from industry organizations and reference frameworks like ISO 27001, NIST Cybersecurity Framework, or CIS Controls. These resources provide valuable guidance on proven effective organizational controls.

d) **Relevance and Feasibility**: Assess the relevance and feasibility of controls for your organization. Consider available resources, implementation complexity, associated costs, and potential operational impact. It's imperative to balance information asset protection with realistic implementation capabilities.

e) **Customization of Controls**: Tailor controls to meet your organization's specific needs. Consider your organization's culture, strategic objectives, critical information assets, and priorities. Controls should align with business needs to be effective.

f) **Regular Re-evaluation**: Information security needs evolve over time. Regularly reassess controls to ensure they remain relevant and effective in response to new threats and organizational changes.

By following these steps, you can select the organizational controls best suited to your information system context. Keep in mind that information security is a continuous, dynamic process, and controls must be constantly evaluated and improved to maintain a robust security posture.

How to Implement Organizational Controls

The implementation of organizational controls involves several key steps to ensure optimal deployment. Here are some guidelines:

a) **Planning**: Develop a detailed implementation plan (a roadmap) identifying specific controls to deploy, required resources, and timelines. Assign responsibilities for each control and establish a realistic timeline for deployment.

b) **Communication and Engagement**: Inform all internal and external stakeholders of the importance of the controls and the organization's commitment to information security. Communicate objectives, benefits, and expectations associated with implementing these controls. Gain support and buy-in from management, operational teams, and information system users.

c) **Resources and Skills**: Ensure that the necessary resources are available for effective control implementation. Identify required skills and train relevant personnel to ensure successful implementation of organizational controls. It can also be helpful to identify potential blockers, including among stakeholders.

d) **Development of Policies and Procedures**: Create

clear policies and procedures for each control. These documents should outline requirements, responsibilities, roles, and processes to follow. Ensure policies and procedures are accessible and understandable for all employees. Remember that each principle, objective, or rule in your policies should be justifiable.

e) **Training and Awareness**: Provide adequate training for all employees on the implemented controls and information security best practices. Raise awareness about risks, risky behaviors, and the importance of adhering to security policies and procedures.

f) **Monitoring and Evaluation**: Establish a regular monitoring process to assess control effectiveness and ensure ongoing compliance. Conduct internal audits, compliance evaluations, and penetration tests to identify any gaps and take corrective actions.

g) **Continuous Improvement**: Promote a culture of continuous improvement in information security. Periodically review controls and processes to ensure they remain suitable for the organization's changing needs and emerging threats. Engage employees in the improvement process by gathering their feedback and suggestions.

By following these steps, you can effectively implement organizational controls and strengthen information security within your organization. Keep in mind that information security requires continuous effort and vigilance to protect information assets and prevent security incidents.

B. Selection and Implementation of Human Resources-Related Controls

Examples of Human Resources-Related Controls

The following examples of human resources-related controls illustrate essential measures to protect information systems as they relate to HR management. These controls should be tailored to each organization's specific needs, considering size, industry, regulatory requirements, and internal culture.

- **Background Checks**: Conduct background checks for all new employees, particularly those with access to sensitive information. This ensures their reliability and minimizes risks of malicious behavior.
- **Access and Rights Management**: Establish processes to manage access to systems, data, and secure areas. This includes assigning appropriate access rights based on each employee's needs and quickly revoking access when roles change or employees leave the company.
- **Information Security Awareness**: Organize regular information security awareness programs for all employees, covering best practices, password management, sensitive data protection, phishing detection, and other threats.
- **Confidentiality and Resource Use Policy**: Develop and communicate a clear policy on the use of IT resources, mobile devices, and company communication systems, including guidelines on information confidentiality, appropriate resource use, and restrictions on personal activities.
- **Employee Exit Management**: Implement procedures to promptly deactivate access for departing employees, retrieve company equipment (computers, badges, tokens, etc.), revoke access rights, and delete user accounts.
- **Telecommuting and BYOD Policy**: Establish clear rules for employees working remotely or using personal devices, including specific security requirements like using secure VPN connections and encryption software on personal devices to access company information.
- **Confidentiality and Non-Disclosure**

Agreements: Require employees to sign confidentiality and non-disclosure agreements to protect the organization's sensitive information, emphasizing data protection and outlining consequences for breaches.

- **Security Incident Reporting Process**: Provide a mechanism for employees to confidentially report potential security incidents or policy violations without fear of reprisal.

It's important to note that HR-related controls should extend beyond permanent employees to cover other users with access to information systems and sensitive data, such as freelancers, consultants, and contractors.

Even if these users are managed by departments other than HR, they must adhere to the organization's information security policies and measures. This may include controls such as limited access to systems, confidentiality agreements, or specific security clauses in contracts, along with appropriate security training and awareness programs for these users. A comprehensive approach to user management ensures that anyone interacting with the organization's resources and data complies with established security requirements.

How to Choose Human Resources-Related Controls

Choosing appropriate HR-related controls depends on the specific information security needs of your organization. Here are some guidelines to help you select the right controls:

a) **Risk Assessment**: Begin by assessing information security risks associated with HR. Identify vulnerabilities and specific threats linked to employees and HR management practices.

b) **Legal and Regulatory Requirements**: Familiarize

yourself with relevant legal and regulatory requirements for information protection and data confidentiality, considering your industry and jurisdiction's specific obligations.

c) **Industry Best Practices**: Consult industry best practices, standards, and frameworks such as ISO 27001 and the NIST Cybersecurity Framework. These provide recommendations for HR security controls.

d) **Internal Needs Assessment**: Identify your organization's specific information security needs related to HR, considering company size, activity type, data handled, and employee roles and responsibilities.

e) **Address Specific Risks**: Analyze specific HR-related risks, such as unauthorized access, accidental disclosure of confidential information, or data theft by employees. Select controls that target these specific risks, like data theft before departure or unauthorized monitoring.

f) **Balance Security and Productivity**: Strike a balance between implementing rigorous controls and maintaining employee productivity and satisfaction. Controls should protect sensitive information while allowing employees to perform their tasks effectively.

g) **Training and Awareness**: View employee awareness and training as essential controls. Provide regular training on security best practices, company policies, and HR security procedures.

h) **Continuous Evaluation**: After implementing controls, regularly evaluate their effectiveness. Conduct internal audits, compliance assessments, and employee satisfaction surveys to identify any gaps and take corrective actions.

By combining these factors and adapting controls to your organization's specific needs, you can select the HR-related controls best suited to ensure information security. Remember that information security is an ongoing process that requires constant vigilance and adaptation to technological advancements and emerging threats.

How to Implement Human Resources-Related Controls

Implementing HR-related controls involves several key steps. Here are some tips to guide you through the process:

a) **Needs Assessment**: Start by assessing your organization's specific needs for HR-related controls. Identify vulnerabilities and risks associated with current HR practices and determine necessary controls to mitigate them.

b) **Develop Policies and Procedures**: Create clear policies and procedures outlining security expectations and guidelines for employees, covering areas like access management, data classification, password management, and exit procedures.

c) **Awareness and Training**: Establish regular awareness and training programs to inform employees about information security best practices, policies, and procedures, ensuring they understand their role in protecting sensitive information.

d) **Access and Rights Management**: Implement access and rights management mechanisms to control employee access to systems, data, and sensitive areas. This includes assigning access rights based on roles and responsibilities and regularly reviewing access rights to prevent unauthorized access.

e) **Employee Exit Management**: Create procedures for managing employee exits, including prompt deactivation of access accounts, equipment retrieval, access revocation, and a reminder about confidentiality after departure. Many organizations now conduct exit interviews to reinforce security rules even post-employment.

f) **Confidentiality and Resource Use Policies**: Define clear policies on appropriate use of information systems, computers, mobile devices, and electronic communications tools, specifying expectations around confidentiality, data protection, and limitations on personal use.

g) **Incident Management**: Establish procedures for managing HR-related security incidents, including data breaches, inappropriate behavior, or attempted fraud, with confidential reporting channels and incident response plans.

h) **Monitoring and Evaluation**: Set up monitoring and evaluation mechanisms to measure the effectiveness of HR-related controls, including internal audits, regular compliance assessments, employee satisfaction surveys, and periodic reviews of policies and procedures.

i) **Continuous Improvement**: Encourage a culture of continuous improvement in information security. Regularly review HR-related controls to ensure they remain effective and aligned with changing organizational needs and evolving threats.

Following these steps allows you to effectively implement HR-related controls to strengthen information security within your organization. Engage relevant stakeholders, provide adequate training, and maintain regular monitoring to ensure successful implementation and continuous improvement.

C. Selection and Implementation of Physical Security Controls

Examples of Physical Security Controls for Information Security

Here are some examples of physical security controls commonly used to protect information:

- **Physical Access Control**: Implement access control mechanisms such as access cards, electronic locks, barriers, and surveillance cameras to restrict entry to sensitive areas and zones containing sensitive information.
- **Facility Surveillance**: Install video surveillance systems to monitor sensitive areas and detect any suspicious activity. This helps identify potential intrusions and allows for a quick response.
- **Key Management**: Establish procedures for key management to ensure tracking, security, and control. This includes maintaining a key register, restricting distribution, and establishing protocols for replacement in case of loss or theft.
- **IT Equipment Management**: Implement controls to secure IT equipment such as laptops, servers, and storage devices. This may include anti-theft cables, tracking devices, or secure storage for unused equipment.
- **Secure Disposal of Physical Media**: Establish procedures for the secure destruction of physical media containing sensitive information, such as hard drives, magnetic media, or paper documents. This can involve shredders, document destruction services, or certified disposal services.
- **Waste Management**: Set up waste management procedures to ensure that physical media containing sensitive information are properly disposed of. This might include secure collection bins for confidential documents or secure disposal of obsolete storage media.
- **Protection Against Natural Incidents**: Implement measures to protect facilities and equipment from natural incidents such as fires, floods, and earthquakes. This could include installing fire suppression systems, smoke detectors, and backing up data in secure locations.

- **Visitor Management**: Establish procedures to manage visitor access to sensitive facilities. This may involve visitor registration, issuing temporary badges, and supervision by authorized personnel.
- **Mobile Device Security**: Develop policies and procedures to secure mobile devices like laptops, smartphones, and tablets. This can include requiring passwords, data encryption, and remote management in case of loss or theft.
- **Backup and Storage Media Management**: Establish secure management procedures for backups and storage media. This can include storing them in locked cabinets, encrypting them, and keeping an accurate inventory of the media in use.

These examples illustrate some commonly used physical security controls to protect information. It's essential to adapt these controls to your organization's specific needs, resources, and regulatory requirements.

How to Choose Physical Security Controls for Information Security

Selecting appropriate physical security controls depends on your organization's specific needs, operating environment, and the risks you face. Here are some tips to help guide your selection:

a) **Physical Risk Assessment**: Begin by assessing the physical risks your organization faces, such as theft, unauthorized access, fires, or natural disasters. Identify specific vulnerabilities associated with your physical environment.

b) **Regulatory Compliance**: Familiarize yourself with legal and regulatory requirements relevant to physical security in your sector. Ensure you understand any specific obligations you must meet.

c) **Industry Best Practices**: Consult industry best practices, standards, and frameworks such as ISO 27001 and NIST SP 800-171, which provide recommendations for implementing physical security controls.

d) **Internal Needs Assessment**: Identify your organization's specific needs based on its size, geographic location, facility location, types of data handled, and physical assets requiring protection.

e) **Cost and Resources**: Consider budget constraints and available resources to implement and maintain these physical controls. Some may require significant investments in equipment, security systems, surveillance, etc.

f) **Effectiveness and Practicality**: Evaluate the effectiveness and practicality of proposed physical controls. Ensure they address identified risks and are suitable for your organization regarding functionality, ease of use, and maintainability.

g) **Balance Between Security and Operational Needs**: Strive for a balance between security and operational functionality. Physical controls should not overly hinder daily operations and should integrate seamlessly into the work environment.

h) **Ongoing Evaluation**: Once controls are in place, evaluate them regularly to ensure they are effective and meet information security objectives. Conduct internal audits, regular inspections, and penetration testing to identify gaps and areas for improvement.

By combining these factors and tailoring physical controls to your organization's specific needs, you can select the most appropriate controls for ensuring information security.

How to Implement Physical Security Controls for Information Security

Implementing physical security controls requires several key steps. Here are some tips to guide you through the process:

a) **Assessment of Specific Needs**: Identify necessary physical controls based on identified risks and vulnerabilities in your environment. Consider aspects like facility protection, access management, surveillance, and equipment management.

b) **Development of Policies and Procedures**: Create clear policies and procedures outlining guidelines and expectations for physical security. These documents should cover topics such as facility access, key management, equipment protection, etc.

c) **Implementation of Physical Controls**: Deploy necessary controls per established policies and procedures. This may involve installing security systems, setting up access control mechanisms, managing keys, and implementing video surveillance.

d) **Awareness and Training**: Educate employees on the importance of physical security controls and provide training on best practices. Ensure everyone in the organization understands policies, procedures, and their role in physical security.

e) **Physical Access Management**: Establish procedures for managing access to facilities and sensitive areas, using tools such as access cards, codes, and ID badges, and documenting and verifying access authorizations. Integrating physical and logical access management needs can reduce costs and simplify incident management.

f) **Monitoring and Maintenance**: Continuously monitor physical security systems to detect any malfunctions or potential incidents. Perform regular checks to ensure controls are functional and in good working order.

g) **Incident Management**: Establish procedures for handling physical security incidents such as intrusions, theft, or vandalism, including an incident response plan, coordination with relevant authorities, and restoration of systems after an incident.

h) **Ongoing Evaluation**: Regularly assess the effectiveness of physical controls by conducting internal audits, inspections, and security testing. Identify any gaps and take corrective action to improve physical security.

By following these steps, you can effectively implement physical security controls within your organization. Tailor these measures to your environment's specific needs, maintain them regularly, and update them to address new threats and technological changes.

D. Selection and Implementation of Technological and Technical Controls

Examples of Technological and Technical Controls

Here are some examples of technological and technical controls to implement within an information system:

- **Firewall**: Implement a firewall to control incoming and outgoing network traffic, filtering unauthorized connections and blocking potential attacks.
- **Intrusion Detection Systems (IDS) and Intrusion Prevention Systems (IPS)**: Use these systems to detect and prevent suspicious network activities. IDS analyzes network traffic to identify abnormal behaviors, while IPS blocks or limits malicious actions in real-time.
- **Antivirus and Antimalware**: Regularly install and update antivirus and antimalware software to detect and remove threats like viruses, malware, and trojans.

- **Data Encryption**: Use encryption tools to protect sensitive information during storage, transit, and backup. Encryption transforms data into an unreadable format for unauthorized people, ensuring confidentiality.
- **Strong Authentication**: Implement strong authentication, such as two-factor authentication (2FA), to strengthen access security for systems and data. This requires a second identification method, in addition to a password, such as a temporary code sent to a mobile device.
- **Patch Management**: Regularly apply security patches and software updates to fix known vulnerabilities. This keeps systems up-to-date and prevents attacks that exploit security weaknesses.
- **Regular Backups**: Perform regular backups of critical data to ensure availability in case of system failure or data loss. Backups should be conducted on secure external storage and regularly verified to ensure integrity.
- **Data Access Control**: Establish granular access controls for sensitive data by assigning access rights based on user roles and responsibilities. This ensures that only authorized individuals access relevant data (the "need to know" principle), reducing the risk of unauthorized disclosure or modification.
- **Network Monitoring**: Use network monitoring systems to detect suspicious activities, traffic anomalies, or intrusion attempts, allowing for quick security incident identification and intervention.
- **Log Management**: Collect and analyze event logs to identify security incidents, intrusion attempts, or abnormal behaviors. Logs provide valuable information for detecting attacks and responding to incidents.
- **Application Security**: Implement security controls during application development and deployment to protect against vulnerabilities. This can include security testing, input validation, SQL injection protections, and other techniques to prevent application-level attacks.
- **Encryption Mechanisms to Protect**

Communications Between Systems: Encryption ensures the confidentiality and integrity of data transmitted between systems, preventing unauthorized interception or alteration.

- **Password Management Policies**: Enforce robust password practices, including strong passwords, regular password rotation, and prohibiting password reuse.
- **Malware Detection Technologies**: Use real-time malware detection software paired with regular system scans to detect malicious programs.
- **Vulnerability Management Systems**: Use these systems to scan for known vulnerabilities, prioritize them, and apply appropriate patches.
- **Connection Restrictions**: Limit system access to approved IP addresses, reducing the risk of unauthorized access by restricting connections only to approved IPs.
- **Database Security Techniques**: Apply data access controls and activity logging to protect stored data against unauthorized access and maintain records of data access.
- **Backup and Recovery Solutions**: Ensure data recovery capabilities in case of total or partial data loss. This includes measures outlined in the backup policy, integrity checks, and restoration tests to ensure data availability.
- **Mobile Device Management (MDM)**: Implement security policies for mobile devices like smartphones, tablets, and laptops used within the organization. This can include password configuration, data encryption, application management, and dedicated MDM software acquisition.
- **Virtualization and Containerization Solutions**: Use these to isolate environments and enhance system security. This separation of applications and data within virtual or containerized environments reduces the risk of attack spread and impact across the entire system.

These examples illustrate some technological and technical controls you may consider implementing to ensure information security in your organization. It's important to tailor them to your specific needs, data characteristics, and the risks identified during your environmental analysis.

How to Select Technological and Technical Controls

To choose the appropriate technological and technical controls, follow a structured process. Here are some key steps to guide you:

a) **Risk Assessment**: Start by identifying the information security risks your organization faces. This can be done by conducting a complete risk analysis to identify vulnerabilities, threats, and potential impacts on information assets.

b) **Needs and Requirements Analysis**: Identify your organization's specific information security needs. This may include legal and regulatory requirements, industry standards, contractual requirements with partners or clients, and security best practices.

c) **Existing Controls Assessment**: Review the controls already in place within your organization. Identify effective controls and those requiring improvements or updates to meet current needs.

d) **Research of Best Practices**: Familiarize yourself with information security best practices and recognized standards, such as ISO 27001, NIST SP 800-53, and other reference guides. Identify the recommended controls that best match your needs.

e) **Feasibility Assessment**: Evaluate the feasibility of implementing the proposed controls, considering available resources, budget, necessary technical skills, and potential operational constraints.

f) **Prioritization of Controls**: Rank controls based on their impact on information security and their relevance to your organization. Identify essential controls that must be implemented as a priority.

g) **Planning and Implementation**: Develop a detailed action plan to implement the selected controls, defining responsibilities, timelines, necessary resources, and success criteria. Ensure testing, deployment, and monitoring steps are included.

h) **Continuous Monitoring**: Once controls are in place, monitor their effectiveness and compliance continuously. Conduct regular assessments to verify that controls function as expected and make necessary adjustments as needed.

Selecting technological and technical controls should be adapted to the context of the information system. Every organization has unique needs and constraints, so it's essential to evaluate available options and select controls that provide the best level of security while being feasible and relevant to your organization.

How to Implement Technological and Technical Controls

To effectively implement technological and technical controls, you can follow these steps:

a) **Planning**: Develop a detailed roadmap for implementing controls, identifying resources, timelines, responsibilities, and key process steps.

b) **Design**: Design an appropriate security architecture for your technological environment, determining the systems, networks, and applications that require specific controls.

c) **Solution Selection**: Identify the technological solutions and tools needed to implement the controls. Conduct a thorough evaluation of vendors and products to choose those that best meet your needs.

d) **Configuration and Deployment**: Configure security solutions according to control specifications. Follow best configuration practices and customize settings based on your organization's specific requirements.

e) **Testing and Validation**: Perform thorough testing to verify the effectiveness of implemented controls, ensuring they function correctly and meet expected security objectives.

f) **Training and Awareness**: Provide adequate training to your staff on using the new technological and technical controls. Raise awareness about security best practices and measures to maintain a high level of information security.

g) **Monitoring and Incident Management**: Establish a continuous monitoring process to assess control performance and detect potential anomalies or security incidents. Implement incident management mechanisms for a quick, effective response to security issues.

h) **Evaluation and Continuous Improvement**: Regularly evaluate controls to measure their effectiveness and compliance. Identify gaps and improvement opportunities, then make the necessary adjustments to strengthen information security.

Implementing technological and technical controls requires proper change management, coordination with relevant stakeholders, and regular monitoring to ensure optimal performance. Ensure compliance with applicable information security standards, such as ISO 27001, to verify that your controls align with industry best practices.

E. The SOA

The SOA (Statement of Applicability) is a key element of the ISO 27001 standard, which relates to implementing the ISMS. It is an essential document that identifies the necessary information security controls for the organization based on its specific needs and objectives.

The SOA is developed during the ISMS planning phase and helps determine which controls will be implemented to mitigate identified risks. It provides a list of selected controls from the full set available in Annex A of ISO 27001.

Preparing the SOA involves a thorough risk assessment, analysis of applicable legal and regulatory requirements, and an evaluation of stakeholder needs and expectations. It is imperative to choose appropriate controls based on the organization's specific situation and its information security objectives.

The SOA plays a critical role in the effectiveness of the ISMS, as it guides the implementation of appropriate security controls. It provides a clear roadmap for information security managers, enabling them to focus on the controls most relevant to their organization.

How to Create Your SOA

Following these steps, you can create a solid SOA that details the security controls needed to protect sensitive information and mitigate identified risks. The SOA is a key part of your ISMS and helps ensure a structured and effective approach to information security within your organization.

a) **Identify Relevant Security Controls**: First, refer to Annex A of ISO 27001, which presents a comprehensive list of information security controls. Identify those controls relevant to your organization based on your specific needs, risks, and objectives.

b) **Conduct a Risk Assessment**: Perform a thorough risk assessment related to information security within your organization. Identify sensitive assets, existing threats, and vulnerabilities. This assessment will help you determine which security controls are necessary to mitigate identified risks.

c) **Analyze Legal and Regulatory Requirements**: Consider the laws, regulations, and standards specific to your organization. Ensure that your SOA incorporates the necessary security controls to comply with these requirements.

d) **Consider Stakeholder Expectations**: Identify key stakeholders in your organization, such as clients, employees, and business partners, and understand their expectations regarding information security. Take these expectations into account when selecting appropriate controls for your SOA.

e) **Establish Justification for Each Selected Control**: For each control included in your SOA, provide a clear and documented justification of its relevance. Explain how the control contributes to information security, protects sensitive assets, and reduces identified risks.

f) **Obtain Management Approval**: Once your SOA is prepared, submit it to your organization's management for approval. Ensure that management understands the SOA's implications and is committed to its implementation.

g) **Regularly Review Your SOA**: The creation of the SOA is not a one-time task; it must be regularly reviewed and updated. Ensure that you periodically review your SOA to confirm its relevance and alignment with organizational changes, new threats, and technological developments.

F. Using PDCA to Manage Controls

PDCA stands for Plan-Do-Check-Act. It is a continuous improvement cycle widely used in quality management, process management, and information security management.

PDCA is a structured method that enables gradual and iterative improvements to a system or process. Here's a detailed explanation of each stage in the PDCA cycle:

- **Plan**: This first step involves setting the goals, processes, and methods necessary to achieve desired results. It includes problem identification, gathering relevant data, risk analysis, and defining actions to address these problems.
- **Do**: Once the plan is in place, it's time to implement it. This step involves executing planned activities, establishing defined processes and measures, and collecting the data and information necessary to assess the effectiveness of the actions taken.
- **Check**: In this step, it is essential to verify whether the results achieved match the expectations and objectives set during the planning phase. This involves collecting and analyzing data, evaluating results against defined performance criteria, and comparing them with initial objectives.
- **Act**: Once results have been verified, it's time to take steps to continuously improve the system or process. This step involves identifying gaps between actual results and set objectives, analyzing root causes of identified issues, making necessary corrections, and implementing corrective actions to prevent the issues from recurring.

PDCA fosters a process of continuous improvement by promoting a cyclical and iterative approach. Each PDCA cycle is designed to be followed by a new cycle, allowing for continuous and incremental improvements.

Applying PDCA creates a culture of continuous improvement within an organization, emphasizing careful planning, efficient execution, rigorous evaluation, and constant adjustment of activities and processes. It also allows for problem identification, solution finding, results measurement, and maintaining a high level of performance over time.

You can use the PDCA cycle for the "controls" part of the ISMS as follows:

- **Plan**:
    - o Identify the information security objectives you aim to achieve within your organization, such as protecting sensitive data, preventing security incidents, etc.
    - o Analyze information security risks by conducting an in-depth risk assessment. Identify vulnerabilities, threats, and potential impacts on information assets.
    - o Based on the risk assessment results, define appropriate security controls to be implemented, including organizational, technological, and physical controls.
- **Do**:
    - o Implement the security controls defined in the planning phase, including configuring technological tools, establishing policies and procedures, and training personnel.
    - o Ensure that controls are correctly deployed following standards and best practices for information security.
- **Check**:
    - o Regularly assess the effectiveness of implemented controls through testing, security audits, and collecting relevant data.
    - o Compare the results obtained with defined security objectives. Analyze gaps and identify areas needing improvements or adjustments.
- **Act**:
    - o Take steps to improve security controls based on assessment results and gap analysis.
    - o Implement corrective actions to resolve identified issues, reinforce existing controls, or introduce new controls as necessary.
    - o Regularly reevaluate controls and repeat the

PDCA cycle to maintain a high and constantly improving level of information security.

Using the PDCA cycle allows you to iterate through the various phases to continuously develop, implement, evaluate, and improve your ISMS security controls. This ensures that your organization can effectively manage information security risks and maintain an appropriate, continually evolving security level.

7. STEP 5: ESTABLISH AN INCIDENT MANAGEMENT PLAN

A. Creating an Incident Management Process

Creating an incident management process is essential for ensuring an effective and coordinated response to information security incidents. This process enables the organization to detect, assess, manage, and resolve incidents in an organized manner, minimizing damage and restoring normal operations promptly. Here are the key steps for establishing such a process:

- **Define Objectives:** Identify specific objectives for the incident management process. These might include reducing detection and response times, minimizing operational disruptions, preserving evidence for further investigation, etc.
- **Establish an Incident Response Team:** Form a dedicated team for incident management, comprising members with the necessary skills and expertise. This team may include information security officers, technical experts, and representatives from relevant departments.
- **Develop Procedures:** Create clear and detailed

procedures for each phase of incident management, including detection, classification, notification, assessment, response, and resolution. Ensure these procedures align with industry standards and best practices.

- **Incident Detection and Classification:** Implement early detection mechanisms, such as monitoring systems, event logs, and security alerts. Once an incident is detected, classify it based on its potential impact, severity, and priority.
- **Notification and Escalation:** Set up clear communication channels for notifying and escalating incidents. Incident response team members should be informed promptly and appropriately to enable swift action.
- **Incident Assessment:** Assess detected incidents by analyzing their nature, scope, and impact. This assessment helps determine the appropriate steps to manage the incident.
- **Incident Response and Resolution:** Take steps to mitigate the impacts of the incident, resolve the root issue, and restore affected services. This may include isolating compromised systems, recovering data, applying security patches, etc.
- **Documentation and Reporting:** Maintain a detailed record of all incidents, actions taken, and results achieved. This documentation serves as a knowledge base for future incident management and facilitates post-incident investigations and analyses.
- **Continuous Improvement:** Regularly review and analyze incidents to identify root causes, recurring trends, and gaps in the incident management process. Use these insights to implement continuous improvements and strengthen the organization's resilience against information security incidents.

It's important to note that incident management goes beyond addressing technical issues; it also involves effective communication with internal and external stakeholders, including employees, customers, suppliers, and relevant authorities. A well-established incident management process helps minimize the negative impacts on the organization and enhances its capacity to handle information security threats.

B. Identification, Evaluation, and Handling of Security Incidents

The process of identifying, evaluating, and handling security incidents is a big step in information security incident management. It enables the detection, classification, assessment, and appropriate handling of incidents to minimize their impact on the organization. Here are the different stages of this process:

- **Incident Identification:** The first step is to implement early detection mechanisms for incidents, such as monitoring systems, event logs, and intrusion detection tools. These mechanisms help identify potential incident signals and report them to the incident management team.
- **Incident Classification:** Once incidents are identified, it is important to classify them based on their nature, severity, and potential impact on the organization. This classification helps prioritize incidents and allocate necessary resources according to their significance.
- **Incident Evaluation:** Each identified incident must be thoroughly assessed to understand its scope, origin, and potential consequences. This evaluation may involve technical investigations, malware analysis, system compromise checks, etc. The goal is to understand the details of the incident to determine the appropriate actions to take.
- **Incident Handling:** Once incidents are evaluated, appropriate handling measures should be implemented to minimize the impact on the organization. This may include quarantining compromised systems, restoring

data from backups, disabling compromised user accounts, etc. The aim is to limit the damage caused by the incident and to quickly restore information security.

- **Incident Recording and Reporting:** All identified, evaluated, and handled incidents must be recorded in a security incident log. This creates a knowledge base of past incidents, helps identify trends and patterns, and enhances preventive and responsive measures for the future. Additionally, incident reports should be generated to inform internal and external stakeholders, including management, employees, and relevant authorities, if applicable.

- **Follow-up and Continuous Improvement:** After incidents are handled, it is essential to establish regular follow-up to assess the effectiveness of the measures taken and identify improvement opportunities. This step allows for continuous strengthening of security incident management capabilities and reduces future risks.

Identifying, evaluating, and handling security incidents are key elements for proactive and effective information security incident management. By implementing robust processes and applying appropriate methods, organizations can reduce the negative impact of incidents and ensure the protection of their valuable information assets.

C. Learning and Continuous Improvement through Incident Analysis

Learning and continuous improvement through incident analysis are essential elements for enhancing the resilience and maturity of the information security management system. This step enables the identification of gaps, the extraction of lessons from past incidents, and the continuous improvement of the incident management process. Here are the different stages of this approach:

- **Data Collection:** The first step involves collecting data

145

related to incidents that have occurred. This includes incident reports, logs, testimonies from involved parties, technical information, etc. It is important to have a reliable and comprehensive source of data for accurate analysis.

- **Incident Analysis:** Once data is collected, conduct a thorough analysis of the incidents. Identify root causes, process failures, exploited vulnerabilities, and human errors that led to the incidents. Use analysis techniques such as root cause analysis, failure mode and effects analysis, or specific methods like Event Tree Analysis (ETA) or Failure Mode, Effects, and Criticality Analysis (FMECA).

- **Trend and Pattern Identification:** From the incident analysis, identify recurring trends, behavior patterns, and systemic vulnerabilities. This helps highlight areas needing special attention and allows for the development of targeted corrective and preventive measures.

- **Establishing Recommendations:** Based on lessons learned from incident analysis, develop recommendations to improve processes, strengthen controls, and prevent similar incidents in the future. These recommendations should be specific, feasible, and aligned with the organization's information security objectives.

- **Implementation of Improvements:** Implement the identified recommendations by integrating them into existing processes, strengthening security controls, providing additional training, updating policies and procedures, etc. Ensure that improvements are well-documented and communicated to all concerned parties.

- **Monitoring and Evaluation:** Establish regular monitoring to assess the effectiveness of the implemented improvements. Track key performance indicators, such as the number of recurring incidents, detection and resolution time, etc. This enables the measurement of progress and helps identify opportunities for adjustments or further improvements.

- **Continuous Feedback Loop:** Create a continuous feedback loop using the lessons learned from incidents to enrich existing processes, improve training, adjust policies and procedures, and maintain a culture of learning and continuous improvement.

Incident analysis helps identify weaknesses and strengthen the robustness of the information security management system. By learning from past incidents, organizations can take proactive measures to prevent future incidents and enhance their overall security posture.

H) STEP 6: MONITORING AND CONTINUOUS IMPROVEMENT OF THE ISMS

A. On Continuous Improvement

Introduction

Continuous improvement plays a central role in the Information Security Management System (ISMS). Its goal is to continuously enhance security practices, anticipate evolving threats, and ensure resilience against potential incidents. This chapter explores the importance of continuous improvement in an ISMS and presents the main aspects to consider for its effectiveness.

The Concept of Continuous Improvement

Continuous improvement is based on the principle that there is a need to constantly seek to improve existing processes and practices rather than view them as static over time.

PDCA Cycle (Plan-Do-Check-Act)

The PDCA cycle provides a structured approach to continuous improvement. It includes the steps of planning, implementing, checking, and adjusting actions taken.

Management Commitment

Management commitment is essential to support and promote continuous improvement. Leadership must encourage a culture of learning and innovation within the organization.

Benefits of Continuous Improvement in an ISMS:

- **Strengthening Security Posture:** Continuous improvement reinforces security measures by accounting for new threats and emerging vulnerabilities.
- **Risk Reduction:** Through regular risk assessments, continuous improvement identifies high-risk areas and enables actions to mitigate them.
- **Adaptability to Change:** Continuous improvement prepares the organization to adapt to technological advancements, organizational changes, and regulatory requirements.
- **Resource Optimization:** By identifying inefficient processes, continuous improvement optimizes, eliminates waste, and maximizes the use of available resources.

Key Practices for Continuous Improvement in an ISMS

- **Performance Reviews:** Regular performance reviews assess results, identify gaps from set objectives, and establish corrective actions.
- **Data Collection and Analysis:** Gathering and analyzing information security data highlights trends, weaknesses, and improvement opportunities.
- **Training and Awareness:** Employee training and

149

awareness of best security practices are essential to reinforce a security culture and promote the adoption of security measures.

Integrating Continuous Improvement into the ISMS

- **Documented Process:** Continuous improvement should be incorporated into ISMS documentation, such as security policy, procedures, and action plans.
- **Clear Responsibilities:** Roles and responsibilities related to continuous improvement must be defined and communicated across all staff.
- **Monitoring and Evaluation:** Establishing monitoring and evaluation mechanisms helps measure the effectiveness of continuous improvement actions and take corrective measures as needed.
- **Stakeholder Engagement:** Involvement of internal and external stakeholders, including management, employees, customers, and partners, is critical to the success of continuous improvement.

Note: Continuous improvement is a foundational pillar in managing information security. By adopting a proactive approach and implementing best practices in continuous improvement, organizations can strengthen their resilience to security threats, optimize resources, and maintain an effective ISMS adapted to the ongoing evolution of the information security landscape.

B. Establishing Key Performance Indicators (KPIs)

Establishing Key Performance Indicators (KPIs) is essential for evaluating and measuring the effectiveness of an Information Security Management System (ISMS). KPIs provide quantitative and qualitative insights into the ISMS's performance, enabling organizations to track progress, identify areas for improvement, and make informed decisions. Here are the key steps for establishing relevant KPIs for the ISMS:

- **Defining Objectives:** Identify the strategic and operational objectives of the ISMS. These objectives should align with the organization's information security policy and contribute to achieving its overall goals.
- **Identifying Key Areas:** Identify the key areas of the ISMS that require regular monitoring and evaluation. This may include regulatory compliance, incident management, security awareness, data protection, etc.
- **Selecting Indicators:** Choose relevant indicators for each key area. Indicators should be measurable, specific, aligned with objectives, and enable meaningful data collection.
- **Defining Measurement Criteria:** Define measurement criteria for each indicator. This may include performance thresholds, rating scales, internal or external benchmarks, etc.
- **Data Collection:** Implement a data collection process to measure KPIs on a regular basis. Data may come from various sources, such as incident reports, security audits, user satisfaction surveys, etc.
- **Data Analysis:** Analyze the collected data to assess the ISMS's performance. Identify trends, gaps from objectives, and opportunities for improvement.
- **Reporting and Communication:** Prepare periodic reports on ISMS KPIs and communicate them to relevant stakeholders, such as management, employees, and external parties. Reports should be clear, concise, and provide meaningful information to support decision-making.
- **Monitoring and Review:** Regularly monitor KPIs and review them if necessary. KPIs may evolve based on organizational changes, new risks, or regulatory requirements.

Note: By establishing relevant KPIs and regularly tracking ISMS performance, organizations can assess effectiveness, detect weaknesses, and take corrective actions to continuously improve their information security posture. KPIs provide quantifiable data to measure progress and justify the necessary investments to maintain and strengthen the ISMS.

C. Conducting Internal and External Audits

Conducting internal and external audits is a critical step in the Information Security Management System (ISMS). These audits assess the ISMS's effectiveness, identify gaps and improvement opportunities, and ensure compliance with standards, regulations, and best practices. Here are the key aspects to consider when conducting internal and external audits:

- **Audit Planning:** Establish a detailed audit plan that identifies the objectives, scope, audit criteria, and necessary resources. Determine the stakeholders involved, the audit steps, and the expected timelines.
- **Auditor Selection:** Choose qualified and competent auditors, whether internal or external, who have the necessary knowledge and experience to conduct the audit effectively. Ensure their impartiality and independence from the process being audited.
- **Information Gathering:** Collect necessary information for the audit, such as policies, procedures, incident reports, training records, compliance evidence, etc. Auditors should have all relevant data to assess the ISMS's compliance and effectiveness.
- **Audit Execution:** Conduct the audit according to the steps outlined in the audit plan. This may include staff interviews, document reviews, on-site inspections, and security testing. Auditors must gather objective evidence to evaluate the ISMS's compliance and effectiveness.
- **Result Evaluation:** Analyze audit results to assess the ISMS's compliance and effectiveness. Identify non-compliances, gaps, and improvement opportunities, classifying findings based on their severity and impact on

information security.

- **Audit Reporting:** Prepare a detailed audit report that summarizes findings, recommendations, and action plans. The report should be clear, precise, and provide sufficient information for the organization to take corrective actions.

- **Follow-up on Corrective Actions:** Ensure that recommended corrective actions in the audit report are implemented within the agreed timelines. Track their progress and verify their effectiveness to ensure identified gaps are properly resolved.

- **Continuous Improvement:** Use audit results to continually improve the ISMS. Integrate lessons learned and audit recommendations into the ISMS's continuous improvement processes.

Internal and external audits provide an objective and independent perspective on the ISMS's effectiveness. They help validate compliance with standards and regulations, identify gaps and improvement opportunities, and strengthen information security within the organization.

D. Management Review Process and Continuous Improvement

The management review process and continuous improvement are essential components of an Information Security Management System (ISMS). This process enables the organization's leadership to regularly review ISMS performance, identify improvement opportunities, and make informed decisions to strengthen information security. Here are the main steps in this process:

- **Planning the Management Review:** Establish a management review plan that specifies the review objectives, scope, and criteria. Identify the involved stakeholders, as well as the data and information needed for the review.

- **Information Gathering:** Collect relevant information on ISMS performance, such as audit results, security incidents, compliance reports, key performance indicators, trends, and changes in the information security landscape.

- **Performance Evaluation:** Analyze the collected information to assess ISMS performance. Identify strengths, weaknesses, gaps, and improvement opportunities. Compare the results with established objectives and regulatory requirements.

- **Compliance Review:** Verify the ISMS's compliance with standards, regulations, and internal policies. Ensure all requirements are met and that security measures are effective.

- **Identifying Improvement Actions:** Identify improvement actions to strengthen information security. These actions may include adjustments to policies and procedures, enhancements to security controls, additional employee training, etc.

- **Defining Improvement Objectives:** Set specific, measurable objectives for each identified improvement action. These objectives should align with the organization's information security policy and contribute to its overall goals.

- **Implementing Improvement Actions:** Execute the improvement actions defined in the action plan. Ensure responsibilities are clearly defined, necessary resources are allocated, and deadlines are met.

- **Monitoring and Evaluation:** Track progress on the implementation of improvement actions. Assess their effectiveness and make adjustments if needed. Regularly check key performance indicators to evaluate achieved results.

- **Management Review:** Hold management review meetings to examine progress, improvement action results, and overall ISMS performance. Make decisions based on the provided information and define strategic directions for continuous improvement.

The management review and continuous improvement process ensure that the ISMS remains suited to the organization's needs and evolves in response to contextual changes and security threats. It fosters a culture of continuous improvement and accountability within the organization, thereby strengthening information security and building stakeholder trust.

I) CONCLUSIONS

A. Recap of Key Points

Here are the major points you should pay close attention to:

- **Understand the Importance of Security**: Be aware of the risks and potential impact of security incidents to motivate your commitment to information security.
- **Customize Your ISMS**: Create an ISMS tailored to your organization by considering its needs, size, and culture.
- **Rely on Standards**: Use recognized standards like ISO 27001 to guide the implementation of a compliant and effective ISMS.
- **Identify Your Assets**: Establish a precise inventory of your information assets to better understand their value and protect them effectively.
- **Analyze Risks**: Rigorously assess the risks associated with your assets to make informed decisions about appropriate control measures.
- **Select and Implement Controls**: Choose suitable organizational, technical, and human measures to mitigate risks.

- **Develop Clear Policies and Procedures**: Create documents that define security rules and responsibilities, and ensure they are adhered to.
- **Prepare for and Manage Incidents**: Anticipate incidents and establish a response plan to minimize disruptions and impacts.
- **Commit to Continuous Improvement**: Adapt your ISMS to organizational changes and emerging threats by continuously assessing and adjusting your measures.
- **Prepare for Audits**: Prepare carefully for internal and external audits to ensure compliance and maintain the quality of your ISMS.
- **Aim for ISO 27001 Certification**: Prepare by ensuring your ISMS meets the standard's requirements.
- **Leverage Resources and Advice**: Take advantage of resources, training, and practical advice to overcome obstacles and optimize your ISMS.

These guidelines will help you create a robust, compliant, and resilient ISMS, ensuring the security of information within your organization.

B. Encouragement to Implement an Effective ISMS

Engaging in information security may seem complex and daunting. However, remember that each step toward implementing an Information Security Management System (ISMS) is a step toward protecting your most valuable assets.

Here are some words of encouragement for this essential journey:

Remember that the initial efforts are worthwhile. Establishing an ISMS may seem demanding, but the long-term rewards in terms of security, compliance, and sustainability for your organization are invaluable.

You are not alone in this endeavor. Numerous resources, training, and experts are available to guide you. Leverage this expertise to gain confidence and understanding.

Each organization is unique. Ensure your ISMS is specifically designed to meet your needs, company culture, and operational environment.

Don't try to implement everything at once. Start with essential elements and gradually expand as your ISMS takes shape.

Management commitment is critical (and essential for certification). Ensure that leaders understand the vital importance of information security across the entire organization.

Your employees are at the heart of ISMS success. Involve them, train them, and encourage their active participation to create a strong security culture.

Stay flexible, as threats and technologies are constantly evolving. Your ISMS should be able to keep up with changes.
Learn from other organizations to gain useful ideas and strategies to face challenges.

Each step toward establishing your ISMS is a victory to celebrate.

Finally, remember that your work in information security extends beyond your organization. By strengthening your defenses, you also contribute to global digital security.

Be patient. Implementing an ISMS is an ongoing process. Be persistent and believe in the value of your work.

Your journey toward an effective ISMS may be demanding, but each step brings you closer to enhanced security and a secure future in a constantly evolving digital landscape.

C. Wishing You Success

As you begin your exploration of information security with *My Easy ISMS*, I would like to extend my best wishes for this journey.

May this book enlighten, inspire, and give you the confidence to build a solid and resilient Information Security Management System. The path may seem winding at times, but remember that each advance brings you closer to digital security and peace of mind for yourself and your organization.

May this book become your reliable guide and companion throughout this journey. Face challenges with determination, celebrate successes, and keep learning. Information security is an ongoing journey, but with the right knowledge and strategies, you can effectively navigate the complex world of cybersecurity.

Happy reading and best of luck on your path to establishing a strong and effective ISMS!

All the best,

Alexandre LIENARD

Other books from Alex

In 49 stratagems, you will discover the essence of the art of warfare, and you will win all the next cyber battles.

2,500 years ago, Sun Tzu issued his fabulous advice on military strategy. Applying the maxims contained in "The Art of War" ensured victory without fail. Nowadays, the theaters of operation have changed. Wars are fought on digital fields, across cables and the ether. But some things haven't changed! And from the depths of the ages thanks to this interpretation carried out by a former CISO, the precious advice of the best strategist of all time: Sun Tzu.

Uncover the pivotal guide destined to transform your approach to information systems security: "CYBERTACTICS: Become a Cyber Samurai and Secure Ultimate Cyber Victories".

Abandon the technical manuals that merely present methods without delving into the underlying principles and opportune moments for their application. In today's relentless digital conflict, it's crucial to penetrate the core of strategic warfare and grasp the essence of cyber combat.